SHE IS STRON

The GREAT CANADIAN Woman

The Great Canadian Woman: She Is Strong and Free III

For permission requests, write to
The GCW Publishing House at:
team@thegreatcanadianwoman.ca

Published by GCW Publishing House and Media Group
www.gcwpublishing.com

Special discounts are available on quantity purchases
by corporations, associations, and others.
For more details, contact the GCW Publishing House and
Media Group head office at the address above.

Paperback ISBN 978-1-9992151-3-2
eBook ISBN 978-1-9992151-4-9

Edited by Christine Stock
Book Designed by Doris Chung
Cover Designed by Michelle Fairbanks

Printed in North America

SHE IS STRONG AND FREE III

The GREAT CANADIAN Woman

KOA BAKER

MELANIE MATTHEWS . TANIA DRIUSSO-BELCASTRO

SARA GLENDENNING . SARAH OZMOND . AMANDA DACOSTA

JULIE BROOKS . GAY MCFEELY . SKY EDWARDS

JENNIFER MCKENNEY . ASHLEY SEELEY . AMY BROOKES

NICOLE CLARK . MARIANNA BONFÀ

Contents

Author Bios

Welcome! We are honoured to have you here. You may be aware that this book is a collaboration in which fourteen authors came together to share their stories. What you may not know is that the chapters in this book are so much more than just stories—they are the deepest truths and most vulnerable experiences of these courageous women. The stories are reflections of real-life chapters in these women's lives. Not only have these women survived some of the hardest moments any of us could fathom, but they are also here talking about them because they have learned how to thrive despite their challenges, and they want you to know that you can do the same.

Through being vulnerable in writing, these women have grown and healed more than they thought they already had. They found freedom from their past that they never knew they needed. They found a voice within themselves they never knew existed. There is something magical about sharing and being vulnerable: It brings us closer together, and it allows for a collective healing to take place. Through their vulnerability, they are paving the way for all people to be free to share their struggles and adversities, without shame or judgment.

Our hope for you, while reading these chapters, is that you see yourself in these pages and that you recognize your own strength, your own capability, and your own worth. You, too, are a Great Canadian Woman.

She Is

Courageous

CHAPTER ONE

FOREVER MISSING

Sky Edwards

June 2, 2017, marked the beginning of a busy weekend. It all began with a twenty-week ultrasound that didn't sit right. It was long and quiet, and the technician who started off warm became distant. She was very focused and kept leaving the room, only to come back and do more scans. She invited my husband to come in and then gave us a long and thorough showing of our baby, which eased some of my nerves. She looked perfect on the screen, but the words that followed my husband's question of "Does everything look good?" had me on edge. It was such a simple question. The technician's answer, though true in theory, left me with an unsettled feeling. "I can't answer either way." I tried not to overthink it, but the feeling lingered.

We moved on to my oldest daughter's dance recital. The

costumes, makeup, pickup, drop-off and the show were a welcome distraction. My daughter and I then got away for a staycation for her birthday and for some much needed one-on-one time. We stayed at a local hotel and enjoyed every moment together, blissfully unaware of how quickly life was about to change.

On our final morning, we sat at the restaurant and enjoyed a mediocre breakfast. We had a limited amount of time before my daughter needed to be at school, and I had a long to-do list before she would be home. That day we would be learning and announcing the gender of our baby, and I was filled with excitement. But as I reached for my phone to check the time, I saw three missed calls from the doctor's office, and just as I was about to hit redial, my phone rang for the fourth time. I answered cautiously, and the receptionist said that my husband and I had to come into the office immediately to go over the ultrasound results. Panic and fear threatened to consume me, but I had to keep it together for my daughter.

We headed into the office with a sense of doom. I remember saying, "It's the baby. If it was about me, they wouldn't have needed you there. It's our baby." I played the ultrasound over and over again in my head, and I was hit with the notion that maybe the reason our technician had spent so much time showing us our baby was because it would be the last time we would be there without knowing the truth. I felt sick at the thought of it. Everything that had left me unsettled from that day began to sink in.

Sitting in that room and waiting for our doctor felt like an eternity. When she walked in, I stared at her with an urgent need to know. I needed to know why I was there. What was so important that it couldn't wait? My sense of dread longed to be extinguished. Her face said it all, and yet I needed more. Then her words began to flow . . .

Brain abnormality. Further testing. Vancouver Women's Hospital. Doesn't look good. That's when the world went fuzzy and everything else sounded muffled. I placed my hand on my belly. Not my baby. Not this baby. My husband had many questions, but I had checked out. I didn't want to be there, and I didn't want to hear anything else. My worst fear had already been confirmed. My baby wasn't okay, and I just wanted to go home and pretend it was all just one really bad dream.

I still don't recall the drive home from that appointment. I remember an all-consuming numbness as if my body and mind had shut down, unable to process everything that was occurring and everything that was about to take place. I had so many questions, and yet nothing seemed to matter. It wasn't until I walked into the house where my parents were sitting that I just broke down into tears while trying to explain what the doctor had told us.

I wanted to muster up hope in my voice. I wanted to have hope, but it didn't seem to exist. Saying everything out loud just made the situation feel that much more real, and I didn't have time to be consumed by it because we had to pack and leave for Vancouver.

We needed more testing. More doctors. More answers.

I felt like I was on autopilot, trying to move my way toward something I didn't want to take part in. All I wanted to do was crawl into bed and pretend I had imagined this whole thing. If it weren't for my husband doing all the work, I would have sat on that couch forever, unable to move or breathe or take the necessary steps forward.

Our drive to Vancouver was mostly silent. I had a hard time focusing on anything besides my fear. I realized that we would be making difficult decisions going forward, and I didn't even know who this baby was. The gender seemed so insignificant until now. If I was going to be making decisions for our baby's future, I had to know as much as I could about the baby. Who was I making these decisions for?

I asked my husband to call our doctor to request this information. He agreed, even though he was worried it would only make everything harder. Because I had suffered a miscarriage before, I knew the love you have for your baby was practically immediate and that love and loss were still heavy on my heart three years later. I knew there was nothing I could do to prepare myself for how much losing this baby was going to hurt. I couldn't even fathom it, nor did I want to.

Girl. This baby was our daughter. My daughter. My heart burst with love and sadness all at once when thinking about my other two daughters and how the day should have been so very different, how we should have been all together celebrating this news instead of separated and in a car hours from home. I looked at my husband and said with all the strength I could muster, "I don't want her to suffer." He scanned my face, and I knew he understood. No matter what, she came first, even if it meant I spent the rest of my life broken. Our daughter came first, and it was my job to protect her in any way I could, something I already felt I was failing at by not managing to keep her from this fate.

We checked into the hotel, and I realized how exhausted I truly was. The next day seemed too far away because I wanted and needed answers, and yet I didn't want morning to come. Everything had changed, and the next morning would change everything again. That thought alone overwhelmed me until sleep finally washed over me.

The next morning, we had an ultrasound with the brain specialist. It was a long ultrasound with lots of photos taken. She pointed out how everything about her was absolutely perfect until she made her way to her brain. That's when the room fell silent. The doctor went to work, scanning, zooming, and clicking photos of every angle. I just lay there feeling hopeless, knowing it would still be hours before we had any more information about what was wrong with our baby girl. I asked for photos, and the doctor gave them to me with a soft, sympathetic smile. I just wanted to be able to see my baby while navigating through the day.

✳ ✳ ✳

Over lunch I found myself looking at the ultrasound photo and memorizing the outline of her face. In my head I kept calling her by the name we had chosen. I looked up at my husband and asked if that was okay, and he gave me a knowing smile and said he had been calling her Lennox in his head too. So, our baby girl had a name. She was Lennox Dawn Edwards, and my heart was happy to know her just a little bit more.

We roamed aimlessly as the hours ticked by. The specialist was meeting with a team of doctors who were going over our baby's scans and medical outcomes, searching for as many answers as they could for us and our daughter.

Finally, we were led into a small room to meet with a geneticist. Two women walked in and introduced themselves. They sat beside us and put some files down. My eyes were immediately drawn to the piece of paper that had a picture of a brain on it. I knew we were about to get the answers we so desperately needed, and I took a long deep breath as I willed myself to stay present no matter what.

One of the women started by asking us what we had been told previously, and her face saddened as she prepared to tell us what was truly going on. She began by telling us that our daughter was missing multiple parts of her brain, meaning that some parts never developed. As she was explaining, she blacked out parts of the brain on the paper in front of us, demonstrating what pieces were missing and what those areas control and their function. She had to take a moment, as I couldn't hold back the emotions that were pouring out of me. I couldn't stop the tears and painful cries from escaping. How could my baby not have a full brain? How could this have happened?

It took everything I had to calm myself and bring myself back to the present. I needed to know more. My husband and I took turns asking anything and everything, and I finally just looked at her and said the only thing that seemed to matter at this point: What chance did she have at living a life? The woman looked at me, and my husband jumped in and asked her to be straight with us. She took a deep breath and told us that if our baby even made it to birth and through delivery, her life would be devastating. That word threw me over the edge. Lennox's life would be devastating. I tried to picture what that looked like, and my heart broke.

I looked at my husband and knew he felt just as helpless as I did. I also knew that we both already knew what had to be done. I let the words slip through my lips through the whimpers. What were our options? She explained that we could do more genetic testing to search for a cause, or we could continue the pregnancy, which would involve being monitored and delivering in Vancouver as our hospital wouldn't be equipped with the tools necessary to deliver a baby like ours, or we could interrupt the pregnancy. As those words left her lips, all I could think of was how unfair all of it was. How was it fair to ask a mother and father to make this kind of decision? How could I? But I knew we had to. My only purpose now was protecting our baby, even if that meant doing the unthinkable.

Once we gave our answer, the doctor started explaining the procedure. I just kept repeating that I didn't want her to suffer, and the doctor's eyes stayed soft as she walked me through everything this decision would entail. I was shaking and terrified at what was to come, but I knew we were making the right decision. I knew it was a decision made out of love, and I knew I had to get through it, but I wasn't ready. I asked for a few days. I needed to get home to my family. I needed to hug my girls. I needed to take a moment to let everything sink in. I needed the situation to not be real, but I knew we were past that.

The drive home was long. My emotions came in waves. I couldn't help but blame myself or feel like I had failed my husband. Lennox was supposed to be healthy, and the guilt that came with that was heavy. My husband just kept telling me that it wasn't my fault, and I knew he felt absolutely helpless. It was happening to both of us, but it was happening inside of me, and there wasn't anything he could do to fix it. I knew he hated that feeling. He's a fixer, but there was no fix.

* * *

In between my waves of emotions was determination, and I was planning how I would use this time. I had decided to make as many memories as possible, even if it felt stupid. I wanted everything I could, knowing it would never be enough. But first, I had to tell my daughters that they would never meet their sister. I had to tell people what was going on and about our decision. I only had a couple days and then I would be facing the hardest thing I would ever do in this lifetime. I would be saying goodbye to our daughter.

Those two days were excruciating. Telling everyone was heartbreaking. We had a lot of support, which was also followed by a lot of judgment. I knew not everyone would understand, but I didn't waver. I knew in my heart we were doing the right thing for Lennox and that unless someone was actually living this nightmare, they couldn't even begin to imagine what they would do or how they would handle it.

I needed to escape, but there wasn't an escape, so I just focused on what needed to be done. We found a photographer who gifted us a maternity shoot. It was an emotional process, but I have photos I will forever cherish. I set up a small GoFundMe, as our last trip to Vancouver had depleted what small savings we had, and I couldn't bear the idea of my husband stressing about finances when he deserved to be completely present during this time. We asked for just enough to cover hotel, transportation, and food, and our community showed up for us. The look of relief and shock on my husband's face when he realized he didn't have to stress about the financial part meant everything. I could see it and feel it. He could finally breathe and give all his energy over to us.

The day before the trip, I tried to keep myself busy. But as I walked into the kitchen, the reality of everything washed over me in an unforgiving way. The pain was so intense that I found myself falling to the floor, screaming and crying uncontrollably. I knew loss, grief, and pain, but not like this. It consumed me in every way. I couldn't catch my breath as the sobs poured out of me and everything began to ache. At this moment, I couldn't help but wonder if I would ever truly be okay.

The conversation between my husband and me during the drive the next day seemed to come and go, and I could feel both of us getting lost in our own thoughts. We talked about how that night would look. I had decided I wanted to stay in the room and write, and my husband wanted to keep himself busy. I understood and honestly didn't mind the thought of having the room to myself for a bit.

We arrived at the hotel and checked in, and I couldn't wait to escape all the people surrounding us. Being around people had proven to be too much for me, as I was noticeably pregnant and wasn't up for having conversations about it. When we got to our room, I found a spot on the couch and pulled out my laptop. I wasn't sure what I would write, but I felt like I needed to. I needed to work out my emotions with the hope of understanding them better.

My husband poured me a glass of wine, and I almost refused. I stared up at him in confusion for a moment and then it dawned on me. It didn't matter. As of the next day, I would no longer be pregnant. Tears rolled down my face as I accepted. My husband knew why tears stained my cheeks, and he insisted on staying with me, but I knew that wouldn't change anything. I needed some time, and I knew he needed it too.

Once the door shut, I opened my laptop and stared at the blank page. I was waiting for the words to come, but I didn't know how or where to start. I sighed and looked at the glass of wine on the table in front of me and decided to take a couple sips. I then began typing, and the words and tears flowed out of me. Twenty minutes and two glasses of wine later, I had written exactly how I was feeling. I had a moment of clarity as I realized what this decision really meant to me. I was taking the burden of life and suffering from my baby girl and putting it all on me. I would suffer for her. I would be broken-hearted and have to live a life with a piece of me missing, and I would do it because I loved her too much to put that on her. I then took some final photos of myself being pregnant. I couldn't help but cry as I looked at my full belly, realizing how empty it would be after the next day.

* * *

Walking into the hospital brought back all the emotions I had felt days earlier. This hospital would forever be laced with the memories of learning my daughter's fate, and I realized that it would be the last place my Lennox would exist. That thought alone threatened to rip me apart, but I couldn't focus on that.

I sat down and waited as my husband checked in. A woman approached me and sat down, and I could feel the warmth and sympathy she was exuding. My husband sat beside me and grabbed my hand as the woman started explaining how our day would progress. The information was overwhelming, and I couldn't help but silently cry as I realized losing Lennox was really happening.

The next step was interrupting the pregnancy, but I first had to sign paperwork consenting to the procedure. I had to pick a funeral home to cremate Lennox, and I had to decide if I wanted to approve an autopsy. The woman left us alone to let everything sink its way in. I cried some more, even though I thought it was impossible to have any more tears. These decisions and words felt so foreign. How was this our reality? We had some time before the procedure, but no amount of time would prepare me for what came next.

We walked into the room where the first step would happen. It was the moment I had been dreading the most. I started panicking, and I wasn't sure I was going to be able to go through with it. Everything in me wanted to scream and run away, but I knew I couldn't do either of those things. So, I lay down. The team of doctors and nurses surrounded me, and my husband sat beside me, holding my hand, knowing how terrified I was. The technician applied numbing cream to my belly and turned on the ultrasound. There she was. Lennox. I could see her, and everything in me shattered. I turned my head away and stared at my hand in my husband's. It was all I could focus on.

The doctor inserted the needle through my belly and uterus, and they began. My uterus contracted in pain as the doctor and the technician argued over top of my belly, trying to locate Lennox's heart. The doctor kept apologizing as uncontrollable sobs left me. Hearing their bickering and knowing what they were trying to do was beginning to be too much, and it would all become my recurring nightmare when all was said and done. I closed my eyes and squeezed my husband's hand. I could feel him struggling and becoming agitated with these two women. They were only adding to the pain.

Finally, it was done. The doctor said they would give it a moment and then check back to make sure they were successful. That word made me cringe. Successful. Successful in stopping my baby's heart.

More tears and waiting. The doctor came back and looked at me with sympathy as she informed us that our little girl was still hanging on. She said they would have to do the procedure again, and that threw me over the edge. I couldn't control the panic attack that washed over me. I was given Ativan to help calm me down.

As the Ativan kicked in, I found myself telling our daughter that she didn't have to hold on anymore, that she could let go and that we would be okay. When the doctor returned, relief and heartbreak washed over me as she told me Lennox was gone. She had let go. There was no longer a second heartbeat inside my body, and yet my baby girl was still inside of me, needing to be delivered.

The contractions kicked in and labour began, and I was emotionally exhausted. I was also in a lot of pain, but I wouldn't have asked for any type of help if not for my nurse. I was ready to feel every moment of physical pain because I felt like I deserved it. My nurse's words and kindness were the only reason I decided otherwise. She told me that the delivery was going to be emotionally painful and that I would suffer enough. So, I had an epidural, and the twelve hours of labour continued. My nurse never left my side, and her kindness and conversation helped me get through it. When it came time to deliver, I was shocked at the insane need to push so that I could hold my baby close. Every motherly instinct in me surfaced.

The doctor was anything but warm or kind, but my nurse was there every step of the way. She treated my very still and silent baby girl with so much care. She weighed her and wrapped her in a blanket for me. She told me Lennox was beautiful, and as I looked down on her tiny little face, I cried and agreed. She was small and fragile, but all I could see was my daughter. Tiny nose, long fingers, and big flat feet, just like her dad's. I couldn't help but smile and cry all at once.

I felt love and loss as we made every memory we could. We took photos, made footprints, and wrapped Lennox up and put a hat on her tiny head. I didn't know how I would feel about doing these things, but I had this need to mother her and be close to her even though she was no longer living. She was still every bit my baby.

Handing Lennox to the nurse and saying goodbye for the last time broke me. I knew I would never hold her or kiss her or have her with me ever again. Leaving the hospital without her went against every instinct I had. It felt wrong in every way, and I felt so empty. Not only was our daughter gone, but so was the entire future we had planned with her in it.

The days, weeks, and months to follow were a whirlwind. I bounced between feeling too much and not feeling at all. I lashed out in anger, fell apart at inconvenient moments, and had panic attacks for weeks. Being around people felt impossible at times. I struggled so much with not wanting to be treated like the mother of a dead baby, yet Lennox's absence consumed every part of me. I needed to talk about her and have her life validated and recognized.

Navigating life after her loss was messy and complicated and really hard on everyone around me. I felt like the whole world kept turning, but for me, everything just stopped. I felt so broken and frustrated about who I was and what my life had become, and I didn't know how to fix it. At times, I wondered if I would survive it.

It's been almost four years now, and there isn't a single day that passes that I don't think about Lennox, that I don't feel like a part of my family is forever missing. I still have moments when my heart breaks at the thought of all of it. There will always be sadness in this reality, but there is also a lot of love. My daughter Lennox taught me so much in the small amount of time I was gifted with her. It'll never be enough, but it's what has helped me grow and change and live in a much more meaningful way.

Learning to accept that I wasn't the same person I was before losing Lennox and having to learn who I would be going forward was challenging. I made a vow to honour my daughter in every way life would allow me. I wasn't really sure how that would look, but I made the decision to keep going because I promised Lennox that we would be okay. That I would be okay. And that is a promise I intend to keep to her. The grief never ends, but it changes, and I continue to change with it.

Sky Edwards

Sky Edwards is a wife to an extremely supportive husband and is a stay-at-home mom to her three living children. She is also a mother of loss after suffering two miscarriages and losing her stillborn daughter, Lennox. She shares openly about her journey through life, love, and loss because she is passionate about creating the space for these conversations to be had. She strives to be authentic and vulnerable online and in person because she knows that compassion is lacking and being able to share and connect is such a simple way to show others that they aren't alone in their struggles. She runs an Instagram account and a blog that focus on self-acceptance, positive body image, mental health, pregnancy loss, and anything else that weighs on her heart. She refers to herself as a self-love activist and chronic oversharer, and she is passionate about inspiring and helping women learn to love themselves at every stage in life. Sky worked in the fitness industry for more than a decade until she realized that true health is more than just physical—mental and emotional health need to be included. She jumps at any opportunity to share through writing or speaking at events with the hope that her passion and story can help inspire those who need it most.

This chapter is for you, Lennox Dawn Edwards—for your story and memory to be kept alive forever. Even though you aren't here physically, you have made such an impact on all of us, and because of you, I have been able to love and support so many through their own losses. I will forever miss you, baby girl. Always and forever. ~Mom

She Is
—— Empowered

CHAPTER 2

MY MOTHERHOOD TRUTH

MariannA Bonfà

As I look in the mirror, I can see a different woman staring back. I am not talking about the deep bags underneath my eyes, or the wrinkles starting to form above my forehead, or even my saggy mummy tummy. These obvious changes are not the ones that have made me different. The changes I speak of are the ones I have encountered in becoming a mother. They are internal, invisible, and raw. Staring at that mirror, I see a woman who has strayed so far from her feminist path. I always viewed motherhood as a rite of passage, one that added an extra layer to my worth as a woman. I never gave it much thought or believed that I would change unexpectedly in some way. I thought that being a young feminist had me exempt from that truth. But life always has a way to teach lessons when we think we know best. My transition into motherhood had a deeper lesson to teach me: disappointment, anger, and perseverance. In experiencing those emotions interchangeably, I learned that motherhood is a choice that I make every day.

To begin to understand my journey into motherhood, we need to go back to the beginning. I am an '80s baby, and unlike my grandmothers' powerless generation, I come from an era where my road was paved by feminists. Women like me were given power and choices. I was reminded daily by family, teachers, and society of the importance of being independent of men, and to aspire professionally. I vividly remember attending my first career day at twelve years old. I was very excited because I could already envision myself as an independent woman claiming the world. I recall the female presenter's last words in her speech: "Girls, it is important to be financially independent because there is no such thing as Prince Charming coming to save you." However true her words were for the greater part of my twenties, they did not reflect my true feelings when I became a mom. I did not care for independence if that meant I could stay home to raise my sons. I chose to be financially dependent on my husband. That single-handed decision made me a different woman. I became a traditional backwards woman in choosing my mommy role. I knew deep down that in choosing this role, I was also letting down the very feminists that paved my road.

I know that without the feminist movement, I would not have a voice and a vote. But a big part of me felt angry with my feminist sisters once I experienced motherhood. I was angry that the obsession to make girls like me equal or better to men had done me a disservice in one area of my life. It forgot to include motherhood in that equation. Where does motherhood fit in my era of power and choices? Somewhere in between a job that doesn't accommodate child rearing and a household that needs upkeep. Guess who is in charge of it all? Mostly me, a woman. I chose to be a mom first, then to focus more intently on my career. I did not want to do both roles at the same time because for me, that would be a suicide mission. Harsh as those words seem, I was not going to accept playing tug-of-war between my children's needs and my work obligations. My newfound position as a mother made me question my stance as a proud independent woman. I felt like I was being coerced by work and society to have to choose one obligation over another. All yellow arrows were pointing back to work, and I was dragging my heels. I knew that I could not physically and emotionally give 100 percent of myself equally in both roles. To declare otherwise would have been a big lie. I knew that there was always going to be one role that would take precedence over the other. In my case, going back to teaching and having to respond to the needs of my 300 primary students would leave me frail and exhausted in the evenings for my children. I knew that work obligations would preside over my motherly obligations because I was an overachiever. I was troubled by the gloomy reality of what

I would become as a working mother. Just the very thought of having to offer my children less to take my place in the workforce infuriated me. As I piled on the anger, the gap between myself as a mother and a feminist grew further apart. I was forming a new identity that did not resonate with simply a feminist model. I was becoming something more, and I had no words to describe that identity.

I never struggled with my feminist identity when I was a young twenty-year-old. My experiences with life and death that I encountered in my twenties showed me how fragile life could be, which was especially true when I was a victim of a school shooting at the age of twenty-one. That tragedy and the fear of not knowing if I would live or die taught me to not take my life for granted. It reminded me to exert my voice and choices. The feminist in me felt aligned with my one moment of life and death. It was the fire that fuelled me, and each time I felt defeated, it reminded me that I was a woman who had survived death. I grabbed onto that identity and made it my mission to change the things that were within my control. It was a period in my life when my father found me quite annoying and relentless. I preached about female rights and independence and about how he needed to do more around the house. I found it so easy to build my independence. I felt unstoppable, carefree, and strong because I had all the support I needed to thrive. Then, at thirty years old, I became a mother and was no longer a radiant and independent woman. Instead, I was a disenchanted millennial woman facing the reality of having to juggle all the things I had newly acquired: home, career, and childcare. I felt deceived. I did not want to give 100 percent of myself to work and 80 percent of my parenting responsibility to a daycare teacher. I lacked support in motherhood; the systems in place were not shaped for old-fashioned women like me. My motherhood experience was merely organized to survive and not thrive.

The notion of being a stay-at-home mom began to take root shortly after I had my firstborn. During pregnancy, I had assumed that I would be comfortable to resume work by the time my son turned one. When that time arrived, I simply couldn't do it because I did not want to be independent of him. All those years in school and fancy diplomas could not prepare me for my overwhelming maternal need: codependency. I wanted more time to be with him. I wanted to actively raise him. I wanted to see his first steps. I wanted to be absorbed by all that motherhood had to offer me. For me, motherhood is something deeper. It is unlike any career I have ever had. It does not have a beginning or an end. It is an infinite job that evolves and revolves around my children's needs as they grow. It gives me a deeper purpose to my life, and as corny as that may sound, I am not apologetic. My newfound experiences in mothering had me baffled because I was trained to be independent and unattached, but that did not coexist well with my motherhood journey. My having children created a relationship of dependency. To that, I felt a deep connection. It felt familiar and natural, somehow like a reacquaintance of my female origins.

In my situation, I was fortunate to have a supportive husband who saw value in my being home with my children. His job permitted me the luxury of having a choice. This choice made me uncomfortable because I was well aware of how unrealistic it was for most millennial women to stay home. This lack of choice stung me heavily when my sister, also a millennial woman, became a mom for the first time. She wished very much to find flexibility in her job, so she could balance her maternal needs with her work and financial obligations. But her employer did not feel the need to accommodate her motherly demands, leaving her with no choice but to follow the yellow arrows back to work. Her lack of choice and my privilege enraged me further down my rabbit hole of resentment. I was separating myself further away from the feminist model I was once trained to obey. Those ingrained values were becoming increasingly conflicted with my maternal needs. The feminist within kept badgering me for my mommy choices. It kept poking aggressively, reminding me that I had become the stereotype my feminist sisters fought so hard for me to avoid. My mommy needs steered me right into the motherhood trap, making me and my children vulnerable and dependent on my husband's salary. Despite the high risk I was taking, I was willing to bet on a choice and go against the grain, so that I could live my truth in motherhood.

I always felt in my gut that I would become a mother, but I never suspected I would be a mom to boys. Naïvely, I panicked at the thought of having boys because I was taught that masculinity is insincere, unattached, and disloyal. When I told people that I was expecting a boy, I was reminded of disappointment because I would lose my son to another woman. Moreover, they predicted that I should prepare for female drama because everyone knows that daughters-in-law and mothers-in-law constantly clash with each other. Those perceptions and semi-truths angered me. Why were women maintaining them and perpetuating them in motherhood, keeping them as semi-truths? You see, having been a daughter-in-law, I, too, was guilty in maintaining that semi-truth. For one, I was never taught by my mother how to properly enter and cultivate a relationship with a mother-in-law. Looking back on my earlier experiences in being a daughter-in-law, I entered the relationship as a strong independent feminist, which resulted in pushing away any advice that did not fit into the confound of my value system. If I felt my voice did not matter, I built walls around myself and distanced myself so no one could bring me down. Once I became a mom to two boys, my maternal insight overcame my feministic individuality. It shifted to the importance of collectivity. When I gained that awareness, all battles of importance seized because I surrendered myself to my maternal self. I had misunderstood all along the meaning of collective maternal wisdom. I chose to re-enter the relationship through my maternal wisdom as opposed to my feministic convictions.

This constant having to prove myself worthy and strong as a woman led me down a lonely path after the birth of each of my sons. I struggled with postpartum anxiety. It was an unexpected reaction to my struggles in motherhood. I had never thought that after having a baby that I would feel such intense emotions and vulnerability. The word "postpartum" felt heavy and ugly to me. It suggested that I was a weak woman and an unworthy mother. The thought of being weak and unworthy dragged me down into a black void. My postpartum anxiety was triggered whenever people visited me, or vice versa, because that meant I would have to share my baby. I would plead with my husband to leave me home alone with my baby. I felt this intense need to protect him. I did not want anyone to hold my baby because I felt a loss of control. Anytime someone would hold my son or simply grab him from my hands or a sleeping position, I silently suffered with panic attacks: rapid heartbeats, knots in the stomach, sweaty palms, and rapid thoughts. My thoughts convinced me that my baby was in danger, that he needed me and no one else. Anytime he made a sound of discomfort, I felt my insides tighten like a knot. I simply wanted to take him back where he was safe. Everyone was oblivious as they carried on, but I was paralyzed in my emotional state. I never felt comfortable talking to the people around me because I was judging myself. So, how could people not do the same? In the back of my mind, I would hear my feminist voice sneering at me unempathetically, reminding me that I had freedom and choice that I was strong. She was irked that I was becoming weak in my becoming a mother. People around me interpreted my overprotectiveness as offensive and snobby. Truthfully, keeping control of my baby was the only way of knowing how to cope with that vulnerable stage of motherhood.

My postpartum anxiety diminished completely when each of my sons reached two years old. It diminished because my children became more independent and stronger. Once they developed a voice and could speak on their own behalf, I felt comfortable stepping back. I wanted to allow them their place to assert themselves in the world. I perceived them to be less vulnerable, and my anxiety naturally subsided. I did not consult therapy for postpartum anxiety because I did not know if what I had was an actual symptom of being postpartum. For most of my life, I had only heard of postpartum depression and sadness. My feelings did not fit within those categories. I was not sad or depressed, just overly protective and worried. I only discovered postpartum anxiety after my second son turned two because I decided to explore the topic myself. I was shocked when I learned that postpartum anxiety is considered a hidden disorder. It reflected the way I experienced it. In learning about my type of postpartum disorder, I learned that my manifestations of anxiety were due to a state of hyper-alertness and hypervigilance. These emotional states were the culprit for my overprotectiveness and triggers. In all honesty, I truly wish I would have sought help for myself, knowing what I know now.

I would not have needed to suffer in silence. I could have found the tools to cope with my emotional irregularity.

As Motherhood took hold in my life, she became me. Through her, I learned to experience her woes and joys. Her first woes accompanied me in my silent suffering with postpartum anxiety, whereas her joys took me to a deeply emotional love experience. In my case, I never expected for my children to have such an impact on my heart—to be the source of my joy and sorrow. Both my sons taught me that love is neither feminine nor masculine. It is infinite and bountiful. In this delicate dance between woes and joys, I have also learned the true meaning of perseverance in motherhood.

My eldest, a complicated little person, triggered in me a sense of powerlessness and inadequacy as a first-time mom. As he developed and grew, I encountered obstacles that were different from the mothers of my entourage. I was stuck in a place where no one could relate to my struggles. I would ruminate over questions: Why does my son not like food? Why does he still drool at three years old? Why can't he pronounce his words correctly? Why does he throw tantrums when his pants or sweater ride up? Am I to blame for any of these difficulties? Pondering these "whys" felt like such a burden on my soul because I, who advocated for countless mothers and their children, was lost, confused, and alone in my parenting battles. Naïvely, I did not expect that becoming a mother to a tiny person would entail such great hurdles. I did not have the tools to understand him, which left me with a feeling of great helplessness—the absolute worst feeling for any mother. Unlike Locke's theory that suggests children are born with a tabula rasa, a blank slate, my sweet boy was not a blank slate. He came into this world already packaged with his unique traits, and I simply had to learn to listen to him to learn the best way to unwrap him.

Most moms know when something is different with their child. We call this a motherly instinct, a nagging feeling that just does not let up. My nagging feeling caused me to take action and find answers. It helped me persevere and push forward when I was being told that his developmental issues would self-regulate. It was so maddening to hear my son's pediatrician minimize my concerns. He offered me solutions. But neither the nutritionist nor the physiotherapist did anything to improve my son's developmental situation. I was not getting referrals for the right resources. I was exasperated with the process because every delay I encountered was another battle I had to endure. It was one more reminder that I was powerless, and I hated that self-defeating feeling. It made the feminist in me uncomfortable and the mother in me restless.

When my son started daycare part time, it was suggested by his teacher to see an occupational therapist for his obvious food issue. Before that day, I had no clue what an occupational therapist did. But desperate for any new resource, I decided to consult one in the hopes I could get clarity. By the time my son was three years old, he had been evaluated by an occupational therapist and a speech therapist, and when my son finally received his diagnoses for speech sound disorder and sensory aversions, I felt conflicted. Part of me felt relief because I had the answers to my pressing whys. However, the other half of me was fearful because I knew my son would need additional resources to improve his motor and language skills. His issues would not magically disappear without my interventions.

In my son's case, he relied on services to help him develop those delayed skills. Due to his food aversions, he did not establish proper oral motor skills, meaning he had a difficult time controlling his mouth mobility. Also because of the food aversions, his fine motor skills were delayed since he did not like to play with textures and food. On top of those issues, he struggled with word pronunciations and saliva-tongue control. Things that should have been simple were complicated: talking, eating, and dressing resulted in cringing tantrums. I knew full well that if I were back at work, I would be only entitled to a handful of paid parental absences. Additionally, my profession, unlike my husband's, did not provide insurance for these types of services, leaving me even more dependent on my spouse.

As a mother, I wanted my child to thrive. I knew that he would need my guidance to overcome his obstacles to succeed in school. But I never thought his issues would become my sole purpose. His issues became my own, tied in with my own identity and my responsibilities. That codependency felt heavy, but natural—how could it not? I carried him in my tummy for forty-two weeks.

We had obstacles when sharing a body with different needs and growing together, like when he kicked or gave me heartburn. I, the gatekeeper to his life.

On the other hand, the feminist within me needed to save him from the negative boy stereotype. I knew very well that if he struggled with his delayed skills, he would create a negative association to school, which would set a precedence for the rest of his academic journey. My deepest fear was that he would become a high school dropout. This intensity that I created was a reflection of my need to overachieve and excel as a mother. The feminist within me was creeping into my motherly duties. I was scared of failure. I was scared to have a son who would become the boy stereotype—the one I was trained to fight and surpass. The mother within could not survive this outcome. At all costs, I wanted him on my side, the matriarch's side, and dismantling the patriarchy.

In my pursuit to aid my son, I felt disheartened as his mother because I had acquired an invisible responsibility that my profession did not accommodate. That invisibility factor scared me because it showed me that there was no truth in motherhood. Feminism made space for me as a woman sitting at the table. But it did not make space for me, the mother, or my child, my codependent. It showed me that feminism had its hand in making childcare a woman's problem, and that was the final straw that broke me away from my feminist self. I felt ill-prepared for the ultimate sacrifice that child rearing brings forth. More specifically, how much care children truly require and what that entails for me on an emotional level as the mother. My son's ten fingers and ten toes were just the tip of the iceberg. For me, they were the awakening of my femininity and my pursuit of truth in motherhood. They set me on a mominist mission—the quest to fight for my mom rights and my children's rights.

In this quest for truth in my motherhood, I had to define that part of me that was a mominist and not a feminist. A feminist speaks about women's rights, but a mominist advocates for the needs of mothers and children and includes a seat at her table for them. She was my newly acquired identity. I accepted her with open arms because I was fed up with being angry, invisible, and helpless in my motherhood obstacles. I hated that my motherhood hurdles did not carry weight in society. Instead, it compressed me and my child into a tin can. I felt I had the responsibility to speak out on behalf of my son's issues and my struggles because in doing so, it would release my truth. It would allow me to claim back my power as a mominist. A mom with a child.

The first thing I did for myself was eliminate personal social media accounts that negatively targeted my self-esteem as a mother and woman. For one, those superficial accounts knocked me down emotionally, and they diminished my struggles and truth about motherhood. I was livid and unsympathetic with the way women were unrealistically portraying motherhood on social media. Motherhood was an image of effortless perfection. A big fat lie plastered with wallpaper of superficiality and deception, and I knew that this perfection was not the reality of most mothers because I was that mother. It was the work of the collective female ego projecting a false sense of how motherhood should be perceived to the outside world—one free of invisible disabilities, mental illness, and developmental challenges. Consequently, I wanted no part in that narrative. So, I did what I was trained for as a woman: I used my voice. I used my voice to start my resource blog called OohMotherhood.

OohMotherhood is a web resource intended to help mothers and their children who are seeking a community of truth. I connect women to educational tools and resources because that is how I was able to empower myself during my difficult experiences. I also lacked a sense of belonging and community as I was wavering with my feminist values. I want to belong to a community of women who want to create noise about a truthful motherhood experience. I am infatuated with truth because truth alters reality. I am done justifying that because I am strong and independent, I should just stand up and take it. It is because I am strong and independent that I can step forward and say NO. No to the invisible motherload. Motherhood today is a place of vaunts and complaints because it is lacking truth, truth on how messy motherhood can be, especially if we are honest about issues such as mental illness, domestic violence, suicide, sobriety, and invisible disabilities. If I embrace stigmas and taboos, I can then disempower them. OohMotherhood is me.

In my feminist and mominist battles, my inner women depicted what I was observing on the outside world between women: the absence of female solidarity. I wanted to be a woman that empowers a woman. My hope for OohMotherhood is that it becomes a matriarch hub that encourages female solidarity, that it seeks to represent the true needs of mothers and children and, in the end, betters the lives of women like my sister and me, and their offspring.

Motherhood hit me like a wrecking ball, tearing me down and then building me back up, piece by piece. It demanded more of me, so much more than I was aware of being capable of giving. It showed me my worth in being a mother and not just a woman. I have come to terms with no longer being a real feminist. I have placed her down respectfully, for she served me well in my twenties. To honour her, I have chosen to take a branch from her and apply all that she has taught me in motherhood. Today, I am a mominist. I reserve my fight for my motherly rights and those of my children because we are one. Motherhood is a choice I make every day, and I plan to do it with truth and integrity. In return, I ask for every single woman to show solidarity by extending themselves genuinely. I encourage you to reach for another woman and offer a hand of gratitude, a truthful word, and an attentive ear. If we could collectively breathe a new truth into our motherhood experiences, imagine all the good that can transpire for the next generations concerning family policies, education, sexual assault laws, global warming, and war. Our momininity holds the key to unlocking so many closed doors. But we can only do so by being united and truthful.

MariannA Bonfà

MariannA Bonfà is an avid mother-child advocate, caseworker, teacher, and creator of Oohmotherhood.com. Her passion for helping mothers and children began in her youth through the White Ribbon Campaign. Her diploma in social services provided her experiences with NGOs and Youth Protection and eventually fulfilled her case-worker role for Big Brothers Big Sisters of Montreal. In 2014, she transitioned to teaching English as a Second Language in Quebec primary schools. She advocates for mothers and children on her blog, Oohmotherhood.com where she promotes female solidarity and empowers mothers through resources and education.

I dedicate this chapter to my husband and my two sons. My love, David, thank you for your support in caring for our boys while I spent intense hours at my computer. Thank you for reading my early drafts and for making my voice matter. To my sons, without you there would never be a story. You are my voice, my reason, my heart.

With love and gratitude,

MariannA, aka Mamma

She Is

——— Worthy

CHAPTER 3

I WAS ALWAYS ENOUGH

Ashley Seeley

My kitchen floor—the place where it all started. The floor of the home we had dreamt about together. The home that we would put our love, sweat, tears, and dreams into for twelve years. The place where we would raise our children and where they would take their first steps, read their first books, and fill each room with their individual love and laughter. The place where my spouse and I would love our children together unconditionally, where we would tuck them into bed at night and enjoy Sunday morning breakfast as a family. My kitchen floor in our home, the home that would belong to my loving, caring, and whole family of four. Forever and always, that is where it began. There I sat in the place that was supposed to be filled with love and dreams but was instead filled with tears and silence. The tears continuously poured down my face, and uncontrollable, breathtaking sobs escaped my mouth when I dared open it. I felt like I was sitting in a puddle of water and there would never be a big enough rock to hide under. He left.

"If only I would have changed" repeated over and over in my head. They were the words he left me with. If only I had changed. If I had changed for him, then my family would still be whole. My family would still be that picture-perfect family I had longed for. I wasn't enough. I didn't do enough. I had failed us. I had failed him. I had failed. Period.

I had failed to stay happy and open when he needed it. I had failed to see he was struggling. I had failed to find a second job so he could live the life he wanted and so that we didn't struggle financially. I had failed to keep up with my body image so he could stay faithful to me. I had failed to keep my mouth shut and be the people pleaser I thought he and the world wanted. I had failed to make a perfect life for the people I loved.

If only I had known in those days, the days when the tears and sobs consumed me, that I was being given a gift, a gift that not everybody would receive in their lifetime. The gift of self-discovery. The ability to see that I could, in fact, come back from this experience and that there was no giant hole needed. Today I know that his choices / her choices / their choices—that's on them. My choices are on me and me alone. My choices and my life, their choices and their life. Today I know that I cannot forget *me* ever again. I cannot carry what isn't mine to carry. I can love all those

I care for, but most importantly, I can and do love myself too. Never again can I forget how important I am and how worthy of love I am as *me*, even as a mom on her own.

We had worked hard for the life we had. We were raising an AA hockey player who excelled in school and a competitive dancer who was known for her firecracker personality. We worked full-time jobs and were proud of what we were building in life. We had family and friends who cared for us. We spent our time camping with our hockey family and taking trips as our family of four. We slowly renovated our house and had big plans to make it our "home." I once had a sign that said, "A house is built with boards and beams, but a home is filled with love and dreams." That was going to be us. We were respected. We sat in volunteer positions for various organizations. We were living a picture-perfect life. The life we dreamt of. The life many people would dream of. But it wasn't enough, and I never saw it coming. We had the desire to keep up with what others had, the desire to have the competitive status in our children, the desire to put what life truly was on the side for the vision of what we thought life was supposed to be: two successful parents, two successful children, a beautiful home, the best of the best. It was the real Canadian dream. Or so I thought. "It," that dream, had a cost. A financial cost and lifestyle-change cost. The "dream" came with life handed to us in a messy little ball—a ball we had to sort through, and ultimately, when the going got tough and the expectations we placed on ourselves became too high, we crumbled. We both learned unhealthy coping mechanisms, and we both struggled to stay afloat.

It was 2018, and overnight, I was alone. There was no more "us," no more family of four. It was suddenly just the kids and me. I had a mortgage, a car payment, and a tremendous amount of debt, and it left me unable to give my children the life they had always had. I was determined to keep the roof over our head that we had worked so hard for, but I could barely afford to feed them let alone give them the best of the best. I was a walking and breathing shell of the person I used to be. My mom cooked our meals so she knew we were eating, my dad helped out financially with the extras, and my siblings spent time loving my children because I wasn't capable of doing it. I got them to their sports, but I avoided the other parents like the plague because I didn't want to tell them I was dying inside. I didn't want to tell them I had failed to change and because of that, my spouse had left me for another woman. I didn't want to tell them that I could only buy one fruit and one vegetable per week for my children's lunches and that we were only able to be at the arena and studio because hockey had been paid for in advance and I could make regular payments for dance. I didn't want anyone to know I had failed.

My son's eyes on that night, the night he heard my sobs from the kitchen floor, they broke me, and they became my reason to get off that floor. There have been two times his big beautiful brown eyes have reminded me that seeing the light in them is what's important. All the other stuff just doesn't matter unless I can see that light. That night, there was no light in them. Instead, I saw fear and sadness, and he was clearly grasping to understand what I, as an adult and as his mom, couldn't understand. The floor, my sobs—they weren't helping anyone. I could sit and cry and dream of holding onto the life we had created, the life we had worked hard for, or I could own what was happening and be the change that I wished to see during my darkest moments on the floor. I decided I had to be the change. I didn't know where to start, or what to do, but I knew it needed to happen.

* * *

Step One: I needed to be open with those around me. I needed to be honest and truthful about my struggles. I needed to say that I didn't know how to cope anymore, that I blamed myself for the way life went and that my family unit was suffering. Until that moment, I had been silently suffocating in the dark hole I had created for myself. Sure, I had been out and about, shuffling the kids to and from sports activities, but I had been hiding how dark life really was for me from those around me. How could someone who lived a perfect life, like the one I used to have, possibly understand? How could they understand that I had known about the other woman and had looked the other way to save my family? How could they understand that I had been lying and manipulating situations, not only in my home but also in the community, to deflect from what was really happening behind my closed doors? How could they understand that I chose to keep accepting that life was just the way it was, even when red flags were slapping me in the face?

I will never forget one of the moments I feared the most: having to tell the people I was closest to about my struggles. I feared the day I walked into my kindergarten classroom and told my teaching partner, the person I had worked with every single day for five years, that my life was a mess—that my spouse had left me and that one of my loved ones was suffering from the effects of alcoholism. I feared her reaction and worried about judgment. I feared telling her that I would need time off to figure out the mess I was standing in. I feared letting her and countless others down by needing to choose myself and my family for the first time ever. Her response to this day is what has given me light. She understood, she had no judgment, and she was going to support me in whatever I needed. Huh. Everything I had feared would happen when I finally became honest and open didn't happen. Instead, I was met with love and support. It was like a thousand-pound weight had been lifted from me and all it took was my honesty. To this day, I don't think she knows how much that moment in time contributed to growth on my path. Her reaction meant that there would be others I would be safe to open up to, and for that I will forever be grateful.

Step Two: I had to admit I was powerless over alcohol. In 2017 I became concerned with the amount of alcohol a loved one was consuming. I believed that it was my job to fix, control, and manage any challenges that may arise in my loved ones' lives. I had a strong desire to control everyone and everything around me. If I had control, if they would just do it my way, then I could fix it. Everything would be okay again. I came to hate alcohol. I became obsessed with counting drinks, checking for hidden cans or bottles, and I would lie awake at night, lost in fear—fear that I had caused my loved one to drink, fear that I would be unable to save them, fear that something uncontrollable would happen. It didn't take long for the toll of sleepless nights and worry to catch up to me. I wondered often if I was just crazy, if I was wrong to worry, so I spent countless hours googling the signs and symptoms of alcohol abuse. I became consumed with trying to fix someone else, and I did not realize that in doing so, I was losing so many pieces of myself. I kept quiet, sharing my concerns with only a few people, but I will forever be grateful for the small amount of openness I had at that time regarding my concerns, as it allowed for a co-worker to give me the contact information for a program that would end up playing a huge role in my life: Al-Anon. At first, I believed I had things "under control" and didn't need any help, but as time went on, I quickly realized I did not, in fact, have things under control. I was carrying anger and resentment, I was blaming and pointing fingers, I was manipulating and lying, I was doing everything in my power to avoid looking inward, and I was struggling to see that that was exactly what I needed. Al-Anon helped save me. It was the place where I learned that I am powerless over alcohol, just the same as I am powerless over anyone other than myself and their choices. It was the place where I learned that I didn't cause it, I can't control it, and I can't cure it. The only person I am responsible for saving is me. Finding Al-Anon allowed me to heal, to know that I was not alone, and it offered me a space to be open while remaining private.

Step Three: I had to figure out who I was. I am Aden and Avalynn's mom. I am an auntie, a daughter, a sister, a friend, a co-worker, a volunteer, and a coach. For sixteen years, I had been a spouse. Suddenly I was questioning who I really was. What did I like? I liked watching my children do what they love, I liked helping out with volunteer organizations and giving everything I had to the happiness of others, but what did Ashley have and who was Ashley?

I received an invitation to go hiking from friends who had been in my life for years, and I wanted to turn it down. If they wanted to know about the chaos in my life, they could just ask me; I didn't need to get lost in nature with them for me to dump my shitty life on them. However, I decided to go, and it changed me. That one small hike, where not a single person even hinted at asking about how life was going, was the light at the end of a tunnel for me.

I realized that I had pushed these people out of my life over the fear of them seeing what was behind my closed door and because I didn't feel worthy of having people like them in my life. Who was I to believe that I deserved friendships?

I never felt like I found my way in high school. I had a handful of close friends, but I never felt at peace or like I belonged in the places I tried to mould myself into. In 2001 I watched someone I cared for deeply get into a car after a high school football game. I remember watching her beautiful blonde hair blow in the wind and feeling jealous because she had chosen to spend her time with someone other than me. She was finding her way in the messy new world of our teen years, and I wasn't. She passed away that night in a car accident, in the same car I watched her get into earlier. I had watched her very last moments on this earth in an unhealthy place of jealousy, and my fifteen-year-old brain blamed myself for her death. If only I had been more understanding of the life she was choosing to live, even if it meant she was outgrowing me, then maybe she would still be alive. I couldn't save her back then, and I couldn't save my relationship, so I certainly didn't deserve good people in my life. But these friends, the ones on the hike, they proved me wrong. They proved to me that I was more than worthy of friendship. They also contributed to my newly found love of self-care. Those moments in nature allowed me to realize that there was more to life than avoiding parents in the hockey arena and the dance studio. I could have moments with friends while hiking, running, participating in yoga, or just talking, and they would have a profound effect on me. I became Ashley, the girl who didn't fear trying new things and being active. I became a person who desired more.

Step Four: I needed to find my worth. Before my separation, I had based my worth on the love and acceptance of others. I based my worth on my spouse of sixteen years continuing to call me his wife. I based my worth on being the perfect mom, the mom who carefully labelled my children's beautiful belongings and worked hard to never forget anything they needed to be successful in their days. I based my worth on being the perfect daughter and co-worker. I lived to please others—if they were happy, then that was all I needed to be happy myself. When my life changed, I found myself unable to get off the kitchen floor. I could no longer give to others in the way I thought meant that they would love me back. If I couldn't give to them like I had, would they see me as a worthy person? Would they love me? My tray was full, and my cup was empty. I had nothing to give, and that, to me, was one of the most terrifying thoughts of all. I loved and cared so deeply for the people around me, but I didn't have the ability to see that I didn't have to give every ounce of what I had to them in order to be liked or loved.

Today I am a recovering people pleaser, but I have had the ability to shift what it means to love and care for those around me. I understand that if I do not give to myself first, then I have nothing to give anyone else. The most powerful part of it all though, is that my worth is no longer based on others. My worth is based on me and me alone. I'd be lying if I said that knowing you are worthy is an easy thing to understand, but I am powerful in knowing that I hold the key to my own happiness.

Step Five: Learn how to love Ashley. I did not like who I was. I did not like the person I saw in the mirror. As a child, I refused to get braces, and as I got older, I started worrying about what others thought of me and began hating my smile, so I covered my mouth when laughing or smiling so people wouldn't see my crooked teeth. I refused to wear yoga pants because someone once told me I had a bubble butt. I didn't want a photo taken up close because of my nose. I hated revealing shirts because I wanted no part of my body seen. I'm five feet, and for a long time I hated my height. Throughout my youth, I longed to be one of the tall pretty girls with a nice small bum and beautiful teeth, and that desire didn't go away as I grew into an adult. I literally hated everything about myself.

I knew I had to change my perspective, but I didn't know how. One day, while in the changeroom of Winners, I forced myself to put on a pair of pants and a shirt that were way out of my comfort zone. I then stood in front of the mirror and really looked at who I was. I had lost so much weight from stress that I no longer could say to myself that my butt was too big, or my arms were too fat, or that I had "thunder thighs," so my only option was to see some good in the person looking back at me. As I stood there, I saw her forced smile and took a photo. That moment will forever be etched into my mind, as it wasn't about my appearance now that I had lost weight, it was about one moment when I liked something about the person in front of me. I liked the way my hair hung in my face and how the outfit had a "cute" feeling to it while it was on my body. My body, the body I had once hated. I bought that outfit, and I still wear it today.

Step Six: Learn to feel. Love, happiness, sadness, joy, all the feelings, they are now mine to feel. To own. I spent so much time just coping, blazing through life at a record speed to just get on with it, that learning to change was a big adjustment. As a little girl, I saw and felt love. I loved the moments after my bath when my daddy would snuggle me, and I loved that when my mom stood with her hand on her hip, it meant she had something important to say. I loved the ever-changing personalities of my sisters, and my baby brother's fiery red hair with the silly little tuft that fell down the back of his neck. I loved the smell of lilacs from the side porch of my childhood home, and I loved my aunt's contagious laughter. I saw love, but as I grew, I began to fear love and became consumed with those things that carry less value. But today, because of my journey, I am reminded of those childhood loves, and I can see things more clearly now as an adult. I see beautiful wildflowers growing on the side of the road. I see ladybugs perched on dandelions in my backyard where I sit and read. I see the sunrise and sunset and the beauty they carry. I love those around me unconditionally, and I have been given the gift of understanding, compassion, and empathy—all things that were so worth the journey. I am not done. I don't believe you can ever be done growing, but I am proud of where I am today.

*　*　*

The lessons and the steps, they felt like tiny little tiptoes forward at a time when everything felt so hopeless and sad, but I now realize they were part of the process. Every small tiptoe can be seen as a step forward in the right direction for me. I became honest and open with those in my life. I admitted that things had become unmanageable, and I needed help. I learned who Ashley was, and not just as a mom. I found worth and self-love in myself, and I recognized that I was being the change I wished to see. Life was hard and messy, life is still hard and messy, but the difference in my life now is that I own it. I own my choices. I no longer live in a place of blame, and I fight every day for the life I want to live. My life was not terrible before my time on the floor; I was content, okay, and satisfied. But living that way left me with no reason to want more—I had no desire to grow or dream. It left me with no wish to change. Instead, I feared change, so I remained where I was. And now, looking back, I never in a million years could have imagined that my life changing seemingly overnight would be the greatest gift I have received thus far.

Today I am Ashley. I am enough. I dream and grow. I support women on their journeys, and I remind them daily that they are never alone. I give what I am capable of giving to others, and I know that I am loved by them for being me. I know that I can only carry what is mine to carry, and I know that I am worthy of the love that others give me, as well as the love I have for myself. I am worthy of living the life I dream of, and I won't stop until I get there. My biggest dream thus far was to write, to share my story with the world, to inspire and motivate others to be the change they wish to see. And here I am, a published author. I will stand on a stage one day, and I will use the voice I kept hidden for so long to bring good to others. I will never stop dreaming.

Ashley Seeley

Ashley Seeley is a registered early childhood educator working in kindergarten. She has a passion for working with children and thrives on volunteering with those who benefit from a little extra support. She is a fierce mother and protector with a gentle and compassionate heart. Through her challenges and experiences navigating life as a single mom, she knows the power of self-care, boundaries, and owning her choices. As a self-love advocate, Ashley is on a mission to help others shift their experiences and their world, regardless of their circumstances. She is here to show you all that change is possible.

To those who always believed in me, even when I had no belief in myself. Thank you for always knowing I would find my way and encouraging me on every step of my journey. To my children, my family, my friends, my co-workers, my acquaintances, and even those who didn't grow with me, you have all contributed to the person I am today and to this chapter. I will be forever grateful.

She Is

——— Free

CHAPTER 4

THE GRUDGE THAT HELD ME

Amanda DaCosta

In the end, I discovered that the joy I was withholding was costing me my own joy.

I denied forgiveness until I realized I was the one who needed forgiving. This awareness changed my experience of life, of myself, and of those around me in ways I never would have imagined. Let me tell you how I came to recognize that the things you think you have control over are actually controlling you.

When I was about sixteen years old, I went to my father's first birthday party. Yes, you read that right. His first birthday party. You see, it was his first year sober. In Alcoholics Anonymous, you celebrate birthdays acknowledging your sobriety. At the party, my father chose a special poem to be read, "The Guy in the Glass" by Peter Dale Wimbrow. The poem talks about how your life is a mirror in which to reflect. The poem's brilliance is that it is not about blame or shame; rather, it is an invitation for accountability. It is a call to reflect on your values and desires and is an examination of your self-esteem. For example, if you were to look at yourself in the mirror, would you celebrate or be full of despair? Other people in your life may think you are a wonderful person who has accomplished great things, but when you look at yourself, you know you are not living an authentic life, and therefore, you cannot be genuinely happy. The praise of others is not important if you are disappointed in yourself for things you have or have not done. There is hope in knowing the person in the mirror is with you to the end. The poem reminds us that you can be your own best friend by being true to yourself and living a life of integrity. Being able to do that is to be willing to be honest about what you see without judgment and be willing to change when needed.

* * *

A copy of this poem was the only thing I kept from my father for more than twenty years. I never knew why, but I could not allow myself to throw it away.

When I was young, my father kept a bottle of Five Star Whiskey on the kitchen counter. I hated the smell of it. It smelled like my dad. Eventually, the bottle disappeared, but only from sight.

Bottles were hidden around the house, bottles my older brother and I found while we were playing. We found them between two-by-fours in the unfinished basement, in the broken couch that was all chewed up on the bottom from our puppy, Dino, and in the glove compartment of the car. There were bottles everywhere, and my dad was almost always drunk.

One night my father told my mother that he wanted to get a gun and shoot everyone in the house, including himself. My mom came into my brother's room where we were watching TV and told us we had to go, then told my dad we were going out to drop off my brother's friend at home. My dad blocked the doorway with his arm and said, "You're not coming back, are you?" She told him that we would and then ducked under his arm. We drove straight to the police station. The police arrived at the house and arrested my dad in the driveway.

My parents separated after that night, and we had to see a court-appointed family counsellor. My mom explained that we were going to talk about no longer living with my dad.

We all sat in a circle: my mom, my dad, my brother, me, and the family counsellor. The counsellor looked directly at me and asked how I was feeling about my dad not being at home with us. I felt my cheeks get hot and my body stiffen. I had a million thoughts and none, all at the same time. I do not know how long I sat there in silence and confusion before the counsellor asked the next pointed question.

"Amanda, don't you want your dad to come back home?" The question came at me like a laser cutting through the silence. It felt as though I were sitting in a bright spotlight, and I felt all eyes on me. My body started receding, slowly moving away from everyone while getting smaller and smaller.

What a loaded question. How could I really say anything other than yes? That was the expected answer, right? Even at eleven years old, I knew there was only one correct answer, but it was not the answer I wanted to give. It was not my answer, but it was what the counsellor wanted, even expected me to say.

I wanted to say, "No! I don't want my dad in the house, drunk. I don't want to see him staggering around, listen to him slurring his words, or watch him eating with his eyes closed because he is almost passed out. I don't want to hear angry voices at night as I lie in bed with all my stuffed animals crowded tight around me." My dad, infuriated, looked across the table at my mom, and it scared the hell out of me. No, this was not the family I wanted back together.

I knew I could not say what I really felt with my dad sitting right there. I did not want him to come home, but I did not want him to know that. I did not want to hurt his feelings. My dad and I had few interactions, and we did not talk very much. How was I going to start saying all these things I was feeling? At the time, I felt caught in the middle of wanting him to go away yet not wanting to be the one to have to tell him. And the counsellor wasn't making it any easier.

"Kids usually say right away that they want their parents to get back together."

Oh, how I wished she would just. stop. talking. Her comment left me feeling even smaller and further away from everyone else in the room. I did not have the answer she was looking for. I sat in my isolation and said nothing, staring at her. My throat was tight and my mouth, dry. I was choking on my own words, words that could not be spoken and would not be for a very long time.

Why would I want someone around who was potentially dangerous but was too drunk to even remember? I realize now that even though I could not put it into words at the time, I felt that my life was not important to my dad, and now this counsellor felt I should care more about having a family than having a happy, safe life. The silence must have been awful for him. Imagine sitting there, faced with the fact that your kid does not want you around. I am pretty sure it was my dad who said to the family counsellor, "I don't think she expected you to start with her."

Thank you! Pressure valve released! Yes, please talk to someone else. Anyone else. And do not come back to me. Not now, not ever, lady. I will just sit here, being small, trying not to attract any attention. If I cannot say what I mean and feel, then leave me here by myself. You adults are supposed to be the ones figuring it out anyway. I am only eleven years old.

I learned that day that I could not say how I felt. In my mind, the family counsellor had already decided we should all want to be together, or at least we kids should want that. Especially the youngest. Me. And in that moment, I became very guarded about how I was feeling and who I talked to about it. I decided that if people did not want to hear what I had to say, then I had to be careful who I spoke to about my innermost feelings. If they already had an idea in their mind about what my answer should be, why do they need to hear my answer at all?

I was also deeply disappointed in these adults, my dad and the family counsellor, for not being responsible. I felt this enormous burden to make things right in our family, even though I had done nothing wrong. And while I was being tasked with reuniting my family, I had no control over it.

It would have been so awesome if someone (other than my mom or brother) would have said, "This whole thing is really crappy! Yes, I see you and what you are going through, and it sucks," instead of "You poor little thing; if only you didn't come from a broken home." What I heard on that day was that being in a family was more important than being safe.

In the end, my dad moved out, and I felt as if a heavy weight had been lifted off me. There was no more guessing as to what mood he would be in when he came home from work. Dinner was relaxing and enjoyable. The house itself felt lighter and brighter, but no one seemed to understand how important that was, and it baffled me.

My parents did get back together for a short period of time. My mother had been under incredible pressure from her own family to give him a second chance, but they soon separated again because nothing had changed. This time we lived with extended family because my dad didn't want to move. One day my parents were having a conversation on the phone, and my mom put me on to talk to my dad. At first, it was the usual questions from my dad: "How are you? What are you doing?" I made brief replies, and then my dad asked me to talk my mom into getting our family back together. Instant tears! I dropped the phone and ran to the bedroom, ignoring my mom's calls as to what had happened. My mom picked up the phone to ask my dad what he had said, and as she was ending the conversation, an extended family member came into the room and gave me a hug.

There was no space in that hug for me to catch my breath. I felt choked again. She thought I was crying because I wanted my parents together, but my tears were from pent-up frustration with the situation. I was tired of being let down by my dad, and I wanted him and the whole situation to go away. My mom understood because she experienced even more than I did. And yet, when I did stop talking to my dad in my twenties, my mom asked me all the time, "Amanda, are you sure you don't want to talk to your father?" I had the same answer every time: "No, I don't. I really don't have anything to say to him."

Throughout my teenage years, I saw my dad regularly. It was

always like meeting with a stranger—someone I sort of knew but with whom I had no real relationship. We never talked about his drinking or about him coming back home.

∗ ∗ ∗

When I was accepted into university, I felt smart, worthy, and capable of accomplishing important things. I needed this validation from a whole university to make me feel significant because I could not find value in myself. I had always felt second to alcohol, and I was just barely beginning to recognize how much that shaped me.

My father agreed to help support me through university because my mother was concerned that she may not be able to afford it all on her own. The day I went to register for my first year, I took my dad with me. We arrived on campus and found the meeting room. I was excited, but my dad looked uninterested. He looked utterly bored, and it deflated me. I did not know at the time how much he had hated school growing up.

Just before the beginning of a new school year, my father informed me that he had no money to give me toward my tuition. Then, a few weeks later, he told me he was going on a vacation. I was shattered. It was a blow—I felt as if I was not worth spending money on, that my dreams didn't matter. I flashed back to my childhood when I needed dental work and my father told me to get a pair of pliers and squeeze my teeth together. It reminded me of sitting at the dinner table with my very drunk father asking me to try not to cough too much because the sound was annoying. I thought about the time he took a drink from the bottle in the glove compartment before driving me to my brother's soccer game. I felt second to something else in his life again, and in that moment, I decided I was done. I stopped talking to my dad that day. It was our last conversation for more than twenty years!

I did not return to university that year because I could not get enough money together to afford the tuition. So, I worked full time and saved as much money as I could because I was not going to give up on my goal to return. Many of the people I worked with told me that since I had dropped out, I probably would not go back, but I decided that there was no way I was giving up on my dream. Luckily, I had the support of my mother and my brother. Their belief in me helped me not give up. I returned to university the following September and graduated in 1997 with a bachelor's degree in psychology. At my graduation ceremony, a family friend turned to me and said, "Today is your day, Amanda. You should be proud of accomplishing this." I looked around at everyone else who was also graduating and said, "So what? All these people graduated too. It's not that big a deal." I could not give myself credit. I could not enjoy the day or celebrate my accomplishments. I did not value myself.

* * *

On Christmas Eve morning 2014, my mother passed away from cancer. My parents had never legally divorced, so our lawyer recommended that we send a letter to our dad, letting him know that our mom had died. My dad asked the lawyer to have us call him. My brother went to see him soon after an initial telephone conversation, but it took me about seven months to see my dad. He had tried to be in touch with me over the years, but I had ignored his calls. Eventually, he had given up. It had been easier for me to push down my feelings and say that it didn't bother me. Not being able to express how I felt as a child shaped how I presented myself to the world. Even as a young adult, everyone saw me as well put together, capable of handling anything, and strong. But the truth was I was more insecure and unsure of myself than people realized. I wanted to be heard without being judged or corrected, and since I had not received that, I shut down, not showing my need for others so that I could not be let down again.

The grudge I had against my father held me and prevented me from seeing and being myself. How did it do that, you may be wondering. Let me unpack it for you. The grudge allowed me to hold onto the anger over being wronged and to continue to feel like a victim by asking and holding onto these questions: Why did I have to have a father who was an alcoholic? Why was I from a "broken" home? Why me?

At the same time, I did not want anyone's sympathy, so I took on the role of a strong person. I wore that grudge like a badge of honour, and I wasn't afraid to tell anyone about it. I realize now that if I had put words to it at the time, it would have sounded like this: "I don't talk to him anymore because he was a bad, neglectful father, and I don't have to!" And, of course, it didn't bother me because I allowed myself to ignore the way it closed me off from others and, even more so, to my own feelings. It was as if neither my dad nor I existed. In my mind, we were both somewhat invisible.

The problem with continuing to hold the grudge for so many years is that its purpose had been done, the situation had changed, as had my father. I needed to re-evaluate it, but I was too afraid to look at myself. The grudge had its hold on me, and I did not know how to let it go. I only saw my father's addiction, his preference for alcohol over me. My mom had been amazing at explaining that my father's drinking had nothing to do with us, and I totally believed her, but it still hurt to be ignored, especially by my own parent. And now that I think about it, it was more than being ignored because that involves being seen, and I never felt that he saw me at all.

I became aware that the woman in the glass was me! That poem that I had held on to for all those years had significance for me. I was afraid to see my dad because I needed to ask for forgiveness. I did not need forgiveness for originally stopping all communication with him, as I still believe that decision was best for me at the time. I needed forgiveness for ignoring him for all those years, for not giving him a second chance, and for not hearing his voice and understanding how crappy it was for him too. It was especially hard knowing he had already forgiven me and only wanted to be with me again. I thought I did not deserve forgiveness because I had done such an awful thing. Who doesn't talk to their own father for more than twenty years?!

Twenty years. That is a long time. It is a life sentence. And I am sure to my dad, it felt like one too! It was hard to look at myself and see what I had caused. This grudge was from the past, and it had run its course. I no longer needed to carry it around with me. I felt no anger or resentment toward my father anymore. The grudge held me because I never took the time to consciously look at it. I never took the time to look in the mirror at that woman in the glass and ask, "Do you really want to keep this up, or do you want to live a different way?"

When I was presented with the opportunity to see my dad again, I felt scared, ashamed, and heavy. I wanted to let that all go. My two-and-a-half-year-old son had brought so much joy to my mother's life. I realized I was withholding this experience from my father, something I did not want to do. Additionally, I was keeping my son from his only living grandfather and, after having just lost his grandmother, what better gift than giving him another grandparent to love him? And the joy extends to me now too as I see how much they delight in each other's company.

By continuing to hold on to the grudge, I did not see how it was holding on to me. I didn't recognize the way in which I was guarded around people and careful about how much I let them get to know me. I had to acknowledge that part of me thought I was such a bitch for not talking to him, and that belief was reinforced by anyone who told me I should talk to him, no matter what had happened! And, at the same time, I needed to show that eleven-year-old me that she deserved to be pissed off, fed up, and disappointed in the adults who had failed her. Even her father. She should not have had to go through all of that.

I had to see what I had done, without judgment. I had to forgive myself and look at the situation as a whole so that I could be whole. The woman in the glass had lessons for me. My dad, family counsellor, extended family members, friends—I had to see them without judging them too. I had to see everything as best as I could as an adult remembering a childhood trauma, which really meant that most of all, I had to feel. I had to let the feelings come up and realize that I would not be consumed by them. And as the feelings rose and I let myself experience them, I was able to put words to them: fear, anger, resentment, disappointment, confusion, and sadness. Those were the feelings I had pushed down, the feelings on which I stacked my grudge—the grudge that held everything down, the grudge that kept me from feeling and having a voice, the grudge that kept me from putting words to my experience so that I could understand and grow from it. Originally, I felt the grudge kept me safe, but now I realize that it kept me small and separate from others. That little girl in the chair who said, "Don't talk to me, don't look at me, leave me alone"—it was time to hold her hand and tell her she was right all along. And now she is safe.

When I decided to stop talking to my father, it was about removing a toxic relationship from my life, but it was also much more than that. Holding on to the grudge gave me back the control I had lost. No one had been listening to me and how I felt, so I gave up talking about it. I wanted to leave it all in the past and move on. The problem was, it followed me. It followed me because it was a part of me. The grudge controlled my actions. It became me. The grudge I held was holding me. And like the weight that was lifted from me when my parents separated, the weight of the grudge was now apparent, and I wanted to put it down. To let it go.

Letting go gave me the chance to express how I felt then and how I feel now. I can stand up with that little girl and say, "This is what I went through, and this is what I learned." This is me. I honour my decision, and I have been able to change how that decision affects my life now.

Since our reconciliation, my father and I have brought joy to each other's lives. We share a love for music, travel, and the beach. We celebrate my parents' Guyanese culture with food and Christmas traditions, which also honours my mother's memory. And a few years ago, I went to my dad's thirtieth AA birthday celebration.

My mother's passing away on Christmas Eve morning brought the opportunity to talk to my dad again. It was a gift from the grave, as if she were asking me one more time, "Amanda, are you sure you don't want to talk to your father?" And this time my answer was "Yes, Mom, I do. I have so much to tell him and so much I want to know about him too."

Amanda DaCosta

Amanda DaCosta spent her career in the mental health and addictions sector as well as working part time in the fitness industry. Having grown up with addiction in her family, she connected with the people she worked with as they struggled and felt shame and frustration over making changes in their lives. Amanda developed a deep understanding for women who were trying to make changes in their lives and face their own demons. She understands the importance of the mind, body, and heart connection. Her approach is to help people reconcile the parts of themselves that feel disconnected by embracing their own humanity while taking full responsibility for their life. Amanda is a well-being mindset coach who works with a non-judgmental framework to show women how to set up conditions for their inevitable success.

For my mother, who has always been an incredible source of strength and grace in my life. I still miss you every day, Mom.

I am grateful for my dad's example of how to overcome an addiction and create a new way of life. While writing this story, I have worried about what people would think of him, and I did not want to cast him in a negative light. I feel protective of both my parents now and want people to understand that they had their own pain and growth through all these years too.

Huge thanks to the best brother ever, for always believing in me.

I am indebted to my husband for his love and support.

For my son, the greatest joy I have ever known. I love you always, Daniel.

This chapter would never have been written without the amazing women of the Great Canadian Woman. Thank you to Sarah Swain, Shannon Miller, and Koa Baker for your support and for urging me to go deeper to find my voice in this story.

She Is

Authentic

CHAPTER 5

IMPERFECTLY ME

Jennifer McKenney

Until you make the unconscious conscious, it
will direct your life and you will call it fate.
~Carl Jung[1]

At its core, this is a love story. On the surface, it sure doesn't seem so. In fact, at first glance, it seems like a cautionary tale on "How to be a Perfectionist and Coping with the Exorbitant Pressure That Comes with It." As I look around me today, I don't think too many women need a how-to guide on perfectionism. Instead, I want to ease this unachievable pressure for you. If you want the short answer: Love Yourself. I know, I know. Easier said than done. The longer answer takes veering off the path a bit and revisiting the fears and shadowy corners of your mind, and for the sake of this story, we will explore mine! These are the places we are visiting. So, this *is* a love story. It's a love story of falling back in love (or falling back*ish* in love—it's a work in progress) with myself and finding my way through the fear and self-contempt that were carefully disguised in overachievement and perfectionism for so long.

I almost didn't write this chapter. I didn't want to. I desperately wanted to back out. Even better—kick me out of it! "Take my money and run," I told the publisher more than once. I got mad at myself. I got mad at them for encouraging me to do it. How the hell did I even pass the application process? My gawd, I was scared.

I self-sabotaged, like I do with many . . . most things in my life when shit starts getting real. I self-sabotage when I need to actually push myself and work through something that brings me great fear, even when something seems exciting to me and is a step toward a goal. The countless things I have let slip through my fingers, or haven't even reached for at all . . .

Two weeks before the final deadline—and I mean third-draft deadline—I realized something. I woke up in the middle of a Sunday night at 3:00 a.m. Holy shit, I just figured it out.

This chapter is the chapter.

This chapter made me look at so many aspects of myself that scared the hell out of me. I was frozen in fear. I couldn't decide what to write, I changed my mind, I didn't know what I thought or felt about anything, and I was almost immobilized in fear at the thought of putting myself out there to the world! Nobody wants to hear from me. I barely want to hear from myself! I definitely don't want to be seen.

So, how did I come to decide to write on this topic? That Sunday morning, I was hit so hard with a realization that I sat up and was immediately wide awake. I had, in true Jennifer fashion, been agonizing over a decision about a job a few days before, torturing myself with what to do, how to manage the decision, the pros, the cons, the money, the potential, how others would feel about it and be affected . . . I thought of every angle my brain could conceive. Every. Damn. One. As I lay down to sleep that night, I asked for clarification. I hoped it would come in a dream, and I'd wake up, not only completely refreshed, but also completely clear on what to do. Asking for clarification before going to sleep was a habit I had recently started after reading about it in one of the many self-development books I have on the go.

That early Sunday awakening was my wake-up call that this chapter WAS the catalyst for me to recognize a very long-standing pattern in my life—a pattern that dictated all aspects of my life, sometimes without me even realizing it until it was much too late, which then repeated the pattern of self-doubt, people pleasing, and self-hate. Ultimately, I was living life in the shadow of fear. Those early morning minutes brought me the clarity to see that over the last ten to eleven years of my life, I have been living to satisfy or impress others, all while trying to see myself as a person of value. Every decision I made in my life was based on how it would best affect someone else or help me avoid putting myself in any kind of awkward situation . . . a task that is perhaps possible in the short term, but impossible in the long term. Making everyone happy all the time is absolutely impossible, but dammit, I'd die trying. But the only thing that it does with certainty is make you lose and hate yourself over and over again until you have no idea who you really are or what you really think. And it's for this reason that I couldn't decide what to write, because I literally didn't know how I truly felt about much of anything. Where did I truly stand on things? I know what I've said, but is that what I think, or is that what I'm supposed to think? Who knows? For years, I've based all my decisions on what other people think or what I think I "should" do.

You alone are enough. You have nothing to prove to anybody.

~Maya Angelou[2]

"What have I done wrong?"
"How could I be so stupid?"
"What should I do?"
These have been my mantras. It's not a pleasant or easy way to live, and my mind never seems to rest. It's an everlasting feeling of exhaustion that is difficult to put into words. Yet despite this obvious fear dictating my life, I have always had big dreams! There

must be more to life than getting up, going to work, and paying bills, then retiring and dying. I have held the belief that it's possible to create a life that brings more joy, a sense of fulfillment, and—the greatest gift I can imagine—a sense of peace. It's been elusive for me, which then brings me guilt because I am fully aware of how privileged I have been and am.

I have generally prided myself on being self-aware, and I can see that I have grown in this area the more that I have worked to take responsibility for my life. Patterns of victimization and blame are easy to fall back on, but once you know something, you don't unknow it! I recognize it now, and that annoys me. You can't feel all justified in your own thoughts when you know you're responsible. No more self-help books for me. Who needs that extra stress? Don't get me wrong—I love growing and learning. It makes me feel empowered, hopeful, and on top of my shit. It's all fun until they tell you that you have to really go within and trust yourself. I don't know how to do that. I stopped trusting myself years ago. The belief that I didn't get much right crept up silently through life experiences and planted its seeds here and there. Eventually, a complete lack of belief in myself moved in, and with it, a turning against myself. So, within my own awareness, I have one HUGE blind spot: I consistently ignore my gut feelings. And now I have lost such connection with myself that I don't even trust the one person you're supposed to trust the most in all the world—yourself! I don't trust me!

"Is that really how I feel, or is that just nerves?" Who the hell knows?! I can't tell, and when I have attempted things, I either fail or self-sabotage, thereby confirming that I had it all right. I just wasn't cut out for it—"it" being whatever it was at the time.

For example, I have made significant (and bad) financial decisions so I wouldn't have to go through the awkwardness of saying no.

- I have bought a house because I didn't want the owners to be mad at me.
- I have taken jobs so other people wouldn't be stuck.
- I have accepted jobs I didn't want because I convinced myself it was the "right decision" and it would build character.
- I have taken on projects, committees, and commitments to not hurt feelings.
- I have bought items because the salesperson spent time with me.
- I committed to a pet because I felt I had hummed and hawed so long that I could no longer say no (I do love that dog though . . .).

And there are many other examples.

I know. Ridiculous.

Now that I look back on all the incidents that make up these examples, I can tell you exactly how I felt at the time. And then I did the opposite. I did it because I did everything for one of three (or all of these) reasons: To prove myself, to make myself worthy, or to make someone else happy/more comfortable.

But, even worse, I didn't follow through on things that I had wanted to do for years and years because I was too scared of what these people, or anyone, would think. I was scared that I would fail at yet one more thing.

You see, failure becomes your specialty when fear runs your life. I became that. And when I became that, I lost me.

This chapter, though. This chapter forced it all to a head. I couldn't get out of writing it. I mean I could have, but I would have wasted the financial investment, and more importantly, I would have lost the dream and one more piece of self-respect. My self-development years have taught me many things, many of which I can regurgitate. One particular concept that punched me in the face is that every time you make a promise to yourself and don't follow through or keep it, you lose belief in yourself and a bit of self-respect. That is SO true! Breaking a promise to another person is taken very seriously, but we don't give ourselves the same consideration. And it matters. A lot.

So, this chapter was a step toward breaking a pattern, but I didn't realize that when I first signed up. I simply saw it as an opportunity to be creative in a way that I had dreamt of for years but was too scared to pursue on my own. Of course, it was those things, but I soon found out it was the catalyst for something far greater. When I first tried to write, I became petrified. And if I could think of a bigger word than petrified, I'd use that one. I didn't want to do it, and I truly didn't think I was ready for it. It was too much, too soon, and too much of a leap. I convinced myself that it would be a better option in the future, or later when I was more "prepared."

My time had come. I couldn't set it aside for later. And to be honest, I was exhausted. So many goals, so many ideas, so many plans, so many failures. It was all too overwhelming to think about and arrange in my head. I was all over the place, scattered, and drawn to the next interest or flashy thing. I had to decide. There was a part of me that knew that this was it for me. If I wanted to change my life as much as I have always said I wanted to, then I needed to change my reactions, priorities, and actions.

I was so excited to meet with Sarah Swain that day in October to discuss my options. What harm could come of that? My husband grimaced when I told him about it . . . he predicted what would happen. I immediately repeated my pattern when it came time to decide whether I was actually going to commit. The "C" word. I tortured myself and my husband all Thanksgiving weekend, then I said no to Sarah and the opportunity. I felt relief. And then regret. Common for me, and I figured it would pass. Except, it didn't. I knew that by saying no I would lose the opportunity to mingle with the type of women I wanted to meet, learn from, and make a part of my life (I'm still convinced I lost that opportunity, but have kept at it anyway). I would lose the battle between creating my life or succumbing to fear. For some reason, this time, it felt permanent. It felt as if I would run out of chances or perhaps just give up because I no longer had any belief left in me.

It's amazing what the subconscious mind can do and how much it controls without us even realizing it. We don't always have the wheel. It takes work. It takes awareness. It takes being gut-wrenchingly honest with yourself. Not fun. It takes being okay with knocking yourself over the head a bit as well as the ability to observe yourself objectively. How humbling. But that's the process of breaking patterns, and it's also the process of self-forgiveness.

Most people looking at me don't see what I see. Or so I've been told. The unrelenting pressure, the lack of confidence, the paralyzing fear that dictates decisions, and the self-contempt even for the most minor of mistakes or human imperfections. But those who have gotten to know me well, and even those who have gotten to know me in this short period of time in the preparation of this chapter, will know what I'm talking about. I'm embarrassed about it. I hope they understand and see the growth instead of the stumble.

Over the years, one of the easiest ways for me to soothe my soul and avoid pain was to simply keep moving. And, moving I did. Different areas of Canada, numerous jobs within my own field, and countless house moves. I busied myself with courses, new hobbies, and daily expectations. I became adept at keeping my mind occupied. Although I considered it adventurous at the time, and still kind of do when wanderlust makes her regular appearance, I realize that I was trying to prove to myself that I was smart enough, fun enough, mysterious enough, competent enough. Overall—worthy.

With age comes life experience! I do believe that life is an adventure and is meant to be lived with some excitement. Wisdom doesn't come from staying in one place or never trying something new or meeting new people. It comes from moving beyond your own backyard. The reasons behind your adventures, though, are what either keep you grounded and in tune with yourself or floating like a buoy being carried by currents.

I did what sounded great and impressive in the moment, as I always believed it was what I truly wanted. I *thought* I was clear. That I *knew*. That I had gone within and it **felt right.** Then reality set in. That familiar drop in my stomach that felt like a thousand pounds, then somehow bubbled its way up to close in my throat. The moment of realization: Shit! This isn't what I wanted! With each of these moments, self-doubt, anger, and dislike for myself grew. "Next time, I'll get it right." But I didn't, because each time something new came up, I looked outside myself for the answer.

"Is that going to make me happy?"

"Am I supposed to feel this way, or am I being a bitch/reactive/too sensitive?"

"I *should* feel this way/do this."

"What should I do?"

I was an expert Opinion Shopper. Not only did it take pressure off me to decide, but if something went wrong, I was justified in my anger for having been led astray.

I asked a psychologist at a women's retreat after her lengthy seminar on intuition and following your dreams, "Anxiety and excitement can feel the same. How do you know which feeling it is? One is there to protect, and one is there to propel. If you are someone who can no longer tell the difference and has lost faith in trusting your gut, how do you know which is which?"

She was baffled and told me it was a good question. She didn't know. It was not the answer I was looking for, but my question stayed embedded in the back of my brain for a few more years. It would be up to me to figure out the answer, and I believe I have.

We know the answer by the feeling we get when we take a moment to check in with ourselves. Really take a moment to imagine the outcomes and feel how those make you feel, then TRUST those feelings. Own the decision and feel the safety and comfort in that. The difference between excitement and nervousness can be felt the moment that decision is made. Which one is it? You know . . . you can tell. Listen to it.

But that takes trust.

So, therein lies the question: How do we start to trust ourselves and trust those feelings when we haven't for so long? When we literally don't know how because we don't know how we feel?

The seed of self-doubt is planted easily and grows like a weed. Any mistake, or perceived mistake, is nourishment, resulting in a crop of anxiety that chokes out confidence. The leftovers, in my case anyway, became a fertile field for self-hatred and the lack of self-respect. How terrible a feeling it is to tear yourself up to make a decision, only to make yourself sick with worry once it's been made, regretting and second-guessing for days and weeks.

All the self-help books say that learning from your mistakes and failures is simply learning. Now, this declaration may stand true for everyone else, but in my mind, I was just stupid . . . I was the stupidest person on the planet. The perspectives of my friends and my husband had no bearing on that opinion. The weight of my own self-judgment was crushing, and to be honest, it was the cruellest of punishments. Although I didn't realize it then, I can now see the link between self-doubt, fear, and my own self-worth.

So, how did that seemingly innocent phone call with the GCW in October about one chapter in a collective author book become the catalyst for conscious change of an old pattern? It forced me to come face-to-face with all my biggest fears: Being seen. Being heard. Being vulnerable. Being honest with myself. And then, as if that's not enough, I had to write all this shit down on paper for other people—strangers—to see. Forever. No control over that once it's done.

"WHAT THE HELL WAS I THINKING?"

I do suggest a good cry. It helps. Just get 'er all out, so it's out, and you can start to be real with yourself.

I had no other choice but to find something within myself to believe in. Anything. The smallest of scraps. Even if just for a moment, to keep me afloat and ground me. Those moments allowed me to pause, breathe, and take a step back. I actively chose to think of situations in my life that I was proud of, or at least decently content with, in some capacity. My ingrained habit had always been to dismiss them and then list out all the things that had gone wrong since and just spiral back. But, since I was consciously thinking, I became aware of that habit and could stop it.

I truly became an observer of my thoughts! Again, easier said than done when we have thousands of unconscious thoughts a day. It takes practice, but with each time, I was able to catch a thought more quickly. It stopped the spiral, which then allowed for a more accurate observation of me and my life experiences.

I started to see myself with kinder, more compassionate eyes—the eyes that my friends and husband saw me through whenever I was lamenting over my stupidity and incompetence. Sometimes it was fleeting, but it was a crack.

As I actively chose to be aware of my thoughts, I became shocked and sad about how horribly mean I was to myself. Sometimes without even realizing it, I'd catch myself berating myself. Once you know, you can't unknow! So, I'd stop it. And if I couldn't say something nice, I would just stop the mean thought and redirect myself. "I'll think about that later," worked wonders for me, and when those same thoughts popped up later, I'd repeat, "I'll think about that later." Later never comes.

But, how does this refocus help you to trust yourself, your feelings, and your gut reactions?

As I got better and better at noticing my thoughts, I eventually found that the negativity didn't happen as often. I was, and am, far from perfect about it, but I have made a lot of steps. So, I gingerly tried something new. I started doing things that brought me joy, gave me a break, or were just damn well what I wanted to do without discussing them with a panel of friends first. I'm talking about small things in the beginning! I started wearing outfits that I thought were more "me," when before I would have said they were too edgy or dressy (or whatever other reason I had). I gave myself permission to not finish a book if I wasn't into it. I allowed myself to rest when I just wanted to sit and *be* and not *do* constantly. I even allowed myself to order the more expensive glass of wine at the restaurant because I *wanted* it instead of sticking to the cheaper glass.

These examples may seem silly or too small to mention, but they weren't for me. They were freeing. I found myself feeling lighter, a little joyful, and even more abundant (just from spending that extra $1.50 on my glass of wine!).

And there it was . . . I kind of started to like myself just a bit. So, I pushed my luck! I made bigger decisions and then started to be a little vulnerable with people. Sometimes it backfired (but I'm pretty sure that's more about them), but most of the time, it turned out well. I hadn't told a soul about this book and hadn't planned to. Ever. But about one month before the final draft was due, I said to a friend, "I have something to tell you."

"OMG! Good for you! That's so courageous and amazing!"

I had been so sure that people would say that I am always taking on too much (true), but more so, "Why would you ever want to do that?" but those weren't the reactions I was getting! So, I told another friend. She was thrilled. So, I told another . . . and then I laughed at myself. What had I been so scared of? I dared to tell a couple friends about my biggest fears about this chapter and what people would think. They didn't make the same leaps I did. In fact, they couldn't even see how I made those leaps at all!

Interesting. Maybe fear can be a little irrational.

*　*　*

I had started a small business in the fall that I had literally been thinking about for years but had been too ashamed to take on. What if I failed and everyone knew? I stepped in cautiously, then quickly found myself running with it, having the most fun I have had in a long time! I have never looked for outside validation for it, and yet I receive it in abundance. I started making the connection that when doing things that bring you joy, you provide service to others, but also, you grow to respect yourself . . . as you! People have been telling me for years to do stuff that brings me joy every day. I thought I had been! But no, my friends . . . I wasn't! You know when you know, and it's one hell of a difference!

The reading and studying of self-development I had done over the years about self-love and self-respect was now clear. I had pursued everything for all the wrong reasons, and I couldn't understand why nothing was coming together. I had only understood the concepts on an intellectual level, but I didn't "get it" because it wasn't until now that I was grasping them emotionally as well. And again, I noticed I was starting to like myself a little more.

As I gained perspective, I allowed my mind to wander to all the past "mistakes" I listed earlier. The most shameful to me. That familiar feeling started to close in my throat. When it was too much, I distracted myself. On days of strength, I let the feeling in and focused my thoughts on remembering how I resolved those situations. How I had lived through them, even when I thought I never would. Eventually, I started to look at what I learned from them and what had come from them. I looked at the perfect timing of some things because I *had* made those "stupid" decisions. The crack widened, and my shadows weren't so shadowy anymore. I forgave myself a little.

As painful as it was at times to remember the feelings I had when I made those past decisions, I now know very clearly what my gut had been telling me. I still get angry at myself as I think of all the shit (and money) I could have saved had I listened to my gut. I had known it all along, yet I hadn't listened. I shut myself off from me. I had failed because I was failing myself.

It was crystal clear . . . after an eleven-year detour!

BAM! Wide awake at 3:00 a.m. on that Sunday morning! "The Awakening." I saw the pattern. I had made every decision in my life for years to impress and please others instead of doing what was best or felt right for me. And I had been under constant fear that I had made the wrong decision every time, and with no wonder! It's impossible to do what's right when not living up to your own potential and gifts.

I had the answers. To the job. To the book. To my life.

And I forgave and loved myself a little more.

Our Deepest Fear is not that we are inadequate. Our deepest fear is that we are powerful beyond measure. It is our Light, not our Darkness, that most frightens us.

~Marianne Williamson[3]

Jennifer McKenney

Jennifer McKenney, at forty-six, claims that she's still figuring out what she wants to be when she grows up! With so many interests, she has found herself to be a lifelong learner with an insatiable quest for self-development and deep soul-searching conversation. A lengthy career in social work has provided her the privilege of working in many different areas of Canada, from urban to extreme rural, and has given her great life experience and perspective. Two coaching certifications have complemented her professional skills. Jennifer gets most fired up when helping others to find their inspiration to follow long-lost dreams. She is most excited when watching women over forty-five find the courage to pursue their goals, no longer succumbing to the belief that it's too late or that they're too old. To best inspire others, Jennifer believes in finding the courage to step into her power to pursue her own dreams and create the life she wants to live, even when it scares the hell out of her!

Alongside the excitement and challenges of significant moves and new jobs, Jennifer has always had a longing for creativity. She has found, after trying many different things, an outlet for creativity through a certification in interior design. She now uses these skills for renovating way too many homes! Additionally, because she is a "foodie," she has nurtured a business that allows for creativity in cooking.

Despite growing up in Windsor, Ontario, Jennifer feels that smaller-town vibes are more her thing, and she has settled (for now) in picture-perfect Prince Edward Island with her husband and two dogs—a miniature dachshund, Isla, and Harry, an aptly named hairless Chinese Crested. Adventures include walking wooded trails, exploring sandy beaches, and biking all over the island with the dogs in their bicycle seats! Reading, dog training, dabbling in a craft occasionally, and time spent with friends in deep belly laughs round out Jennifer's list of favourite things.

*I've put as much pressure on myself with these acknowledgements as I did with the chapter! Why stop being me now? I absolutely would not have even started this process without the unwavering support of my husband, Trent Smith. Even when I think he's not 100 percent sure of my plans, he never wants to dull my light and supports me even when maybe he should slow me down! To my dear friend, Lisa McCormack, who gently pushed through my fear and encouraged me to share my story with her as a first step. She lovingly, strongly, and very humourously gave feedback and encouragement and annoyingly held me accountable. She helped me believe in myself when I absolutely **did not** think I could write this chapter. And, of course, HUGE thanks to Sarah Swain, Shannon Miller, Koa Baker, and ALL the amazing women with whom I am absolutely honoured to be sharing these pages. I am so grateful and privileged (and maybe a little shocked) that they saw such potential in me and encouraged me to see my own light.*

She Is

——— Bold

CHAPTER 6

RUNNING TOWARD THE DRAGON

Amy Brookes

"You can't take her out without me! Something will happen to her!" I cried out to my husband. He looked at me with equal parts concern and confusion. He moved closer, holding our newborn daughter in her car seat. I shook my head wildly, panic in my eyes. How could I explain to him that in the weeks since I gave birth to our child, *I had been living in my own version of hell*? How could I tell him that this love I felt for her was so *big*, so *all-consuming* that I felt if she were out of my sight, something terrible would happen to her?

THE DRAGON WAS BACK.

When I was twenty, after an especially traumatic breakup, I made an appointment with my GP to talk about how I was coping. Not very well, I can tell you. She asked me to go back to childhood and think of my very first memory. I closed my eyes, took a deep breath and was surprised to find a vivid memory come in right away. Me, a little girl, in the backseat of a car, waiting for my dad to come back. I didn't know how much time had passed, but I knew I felt scared. I felt alone, and upon further reflection, I felt abandoned. Silent tears fell and then noisy, big heaving sobs began. How had I forgotten this memory up until now? I didn't need her to tell me why this was so important to how I was feeling. The fear of abandonment. Of loving too much and knowing that that person could leave at any time. I now saw with fresh eyes that I had been living my life in extremes when it came to love.

I've always been a highly sensitive person, very much affected by others' energy. Too little, too much. Full speed ahead or full stop. I felt like a round peg trying to fit in a square hole. I became an expert at hiding, masking, and moulding myself to fit in. I held others at a distance as a way to protect my easily bruised heart. Up until that moment, I hadn't put a name to the feeling I had felt my whole life!

Anxiety, the constant thorn in my side. The sick feeling I got in my stomach. The all-consuming and overwhelming feeling of dread. I'd spent my life feeling like I was in fight-or-flight mode, only I didn't know who or what I was running from.

Anxiety led me to feeling disconnected from myself. It made

me feel different, not good enough, and like I had to pretend to be more like others. Just being me was *never an option*. I viewed being myself the problem, not the solution. I was drained and defeated, and I felt too overwhelmed to do much of anything with this new diagnosis. There was a comfort in my anxiety. It was so much a part of me, and although I knew it had held me back, I also viewed it as keeping me safe.

I held on to it like a life raft and continued to float.

Years later, while at work, I was struck with a very sudden and powerful feeling. It came in quickly and clearly, just as my first memory did in that doctor's office a few years before. It came in like truth and with a deep sense of knowing.

"I AM PREGNANT."

I didn't panic like I had assumed I would. I gathered my purse and walked to the pharmacy on site where I grabbed a pregnancy test, then quickly ran back to my office bathroom and sat on the floor. And that is where I discovered I was pregnant with my first child, one month after graduating university, while in a new job and in a relationship that was on the rocks.

The pregnancy was difficult, filled with 24/7 nausea and extreme fatigue. I felt like I was floating all day, existing only to see the clock hit 5:00 p.m. so I could go home, go to bed and then do it all over again the next day. In my fifth month, I started to feel lightheaded and got headaches almost daily. I was gaining so much weight, so quickly, I felt like I would explode. I remember one particular appointment around this time in which a resident doctor took my stats and commented on the deep red indent lines across my stomach from my too-tight pants. She clucked her tongue as I stepped on the scale and made a comment about my gaining too much weight. I felt a heavy tidal wave of guilt, shame, and embarrassment wash over me. What was I doing wrong? Was pregnancy supposed to be this hard? Soon after, I was told I had preeclampsia—the sudden onset of high blood pressure in pregnancy and oftentimes accompanied with protein in the urine. I was put on bedrest straight away. Although I was nervous about my health, I also felt immediate relief. I could rest when I wanted to. No more 6:00 a.m. bus rides holding a barf bag. I am thankful that this diagnosis came at a time before the internet exploded and became what it is today. Googling information about what was happening to me would have sent me in a complete tailspin.

My now-husband and I had been together for a year at this time and things weren't great. The stress of an unexpected pregnancy nearly destroyed us. I felt responsible for how he felt, even though I knew that wasn't fair. He was trying to cope with his own feelings about this sudden change in our lives, and I was doing the same. Unfortunately, we both tried to cope separately rather than leaning on one another. We each totally shut the other out, and I felt more alone than ever.

I easily slipped back into my old coping mechanisms. I felt like I had to carry the weight of the world on my own. My anxiety told me it was for the best anyhow. I was safe this way. Even in my labour with our child, I felt alone. My husband told me later that he, too, felt alone in the process and like he was just in the way. How were we going to raise this baby together when we both felt so *disconnected from each other*?

My labour and delivery were long and traumatic. I laboured for twenty-six hours and ended up having to deliver with the use of forceps. Despite my body, mind, and spirit feeling like it had been broken, battered, and bruised, when I looked down at my daughter's little button nose and dark curious eyes, I felt hopeful. We were going to make it.

I WAS NOW SOMEONE'S MOM.

During the pregnancy, I told myself I was going to breastfeed, come hell or high water. There was no alternative, in my mind. I don't even know why I was so adamant, but I knew I'd feel like a failure if I didn't succeed. There I was, not able to sit or move comfortably because of the traumatic delivery, trying to breastfeed with a screaming, inconsolable baby. *Great, I can't do this right either*, I thought. My GP, within minutes of meeting my little one, asked me if I'd ever heard or read about high-needs babies. "No," I said nervously. What was a high-needs baby?

WHAT DID I GET MYSELF INTO?

My daughter, like me, turned out to be a highly sensitive person. She didn't sleep a wink unless attached to me. We tried, over and over, day in and day out, to lay her down in a crib or bassinet so I could shower or use the bathroom. Maybe make myself a tea or a meal. That did not fly with her. Every effort failed. Every parenting book lied. This baby of ours would not settle or soothe unless attached to me. When we were separated, her eyes would shift back and forth in a panic. Her arms and legs would flail. The screams nearly broke my soul. No amount of time of letting her "cry it out" seemed to work—all it ever did was leave me feeling shame and like I was a complete failure as a mother. *Screw those parenting experts*, I thought. None of their advice worked for us. We'd have to figure it out on our own. I gave myself permission to be the expert of parenting my child. I can see now how this mindset further supported my idea that it had to be all or nothing, and that I could only rely on myself. *There was no balance.*

Those early days crept by slowly. I was in the thick of it. I was sleep deprived and lacked any semblance of self-care (what was a shower again?). I lived on autopilot. Just existing. I learned to breastfeed with quite a few bumps along the road, but I could never really figure out how to pump, so feeding her was all on me. We suffered through multiple experiences with thrush and mastitis. She nursed all day and all night. I began to feel like not only did

I grow a person but that she attached herself to me with such a force that there was no more *me*. There was only us.

As the months passed, I began to feel that something wasn't right with me. I had no concept of who I was anymore. Less than a year before, I had been a university student, living life for myself. I had had ample sleep and alone time. I had had freedom. But my life had changed so quickly that I hadn't even really begun to process it. I glanced at myself as I walked by our bedroom mirror, and my reflection shocked me. I sunk to the floor and sobbed alongside my screaming baby. I was twenty-six years old and fifty pounds heavier than I had been a year prior. Big black bags rested under my eyes. I looked and felt so much older than I was. How come no one told me about this part of motherhood? *Why doesn't anyone talk about how lonely it is? How can we lose ourselves so easily?* I grieved for who I had been and felt completely hopeless of ever finding her again.

My husband offered help, but I always pushed it away. I see now that I was punishing him in a sense for not being able to help in the way I needed him to. But at the time, I didn't see how anyone could help. I felt equal parts love and resentment toward him. My life had changed the most, I told myself. I've lost my identity. I cannot escape to go to work. I cannot shower in peace or sleep uninterrupted.

I began to realize just how disturbing my thoughts had become. Every single time I closed my eyes, I saw vivid images of my worst nightmares. I'd imagine myself out for a walk, pushing my baby in her stroller and then see my hand let go of the handle and watch in slow motion as the stroller and my baby rolled off the side of a cliff. Or I'd daydream about how nice it'd be to have a long luxurious shower while my baby was asleep in her crib, only to discover that she had been snatched from her room while I took a few moments to myself. My brain screamed at me, *If you let her out of your sight, you will lose her!* I no longer knew who I was without her. She was a part of me—a piece of my heart and soul that lived outside my body. I could not let anything happen to her. I promised myself I would not.

I allowed myself to exist in this hellish mindset for much too long. I refused help from anyone. I'd snap at any well-meaning advice. I believed I was the only one who could take care of my child and protect her from any danger. My thoughts were erratic and nonsensical. I lived in a constant state of panic and fear. I was back in fight-or-flight mode. I can't recall what eventually led me to reach out to my GP for help, but I'm grateful every day that something did. When I was in these moments of distress and distorted thinking, I was completely convinced it was okay, it was normal, and I was fine. I was so completely disconnected from myself and reality. I often imagine my Higher Self swooping in at this time, familiar and loving and offering a life buoy.

"SAVE YOURSELF, AMY, YOU'RE DROWNING."

Months later, diagnosed with postpartum anxiety and prescribed medication, I started to come out of the fog. I gradually began to realize that I had to learn to reach out for help when I needed it. I would pass my baby over to her dad and go into the bath with headphones and a good book. He and I were still living in separate emotional worlds, but I realized that I had to figure out how to adapt. I began to accept that I'd just have to learn how to live with a piece of my heart outside of my body.

A few months before my daughter's second birthday, I discovered I was pregnant again. This pregnancy was so different from the first. I was nauseated a lot but otherwise felt pretty good. I was healthy. I had more energy than I did with my first. My skin glowed and my hair shone. With the help of my GP and my husband, I stayed on top of my thoughts and feelings throughout the pregnancy. I realized that I had felt out of control in my first pregnancy and delivery. I knew that anything could happen, but I felt that if I had more of a say and a plan, I'd feel more prepared. I hired a doula to make sure that I had someone to remind me of my decisions and wishes during the process. I got my wish. I had a wonderfully empowering labour and delivery. I felt like Superwoman. What night and day experiences between labour and deliveries! I was blessed with another high-needs baby, but this time I made sure I was more prepared for it. I got a baby carrier and carried my son around with me everywhere. It helped so much to be able to be mobile. I learned what balance was with this little boy of mine. I learned it *didn't have to be all or nothing.*

I COULD BE A GOOD MOM AND STILL ASK FOR HELP.

I'm not going to lie, it still felt foreign to be away from my kids when my husband took them out without me. My heart would still leap into my throat, and I'd count down the minutes they'd been gone in case something was wrong. But I *allowed it anyhow.* I sat down, looked my anxiety in the face, and gave her a name: "The Dragon." And I told her she was wrong. Every single time an upsetting thought came in my head, I'd say, "No, you're wrong."

Even today, as a mom of a kindergartner, preteen, and teen, I find myself having to stare "The Dragon" down and say, "Nope, not today!" My anxiety is a constant, and I've accepted that it may never leave.

In 2013 we got posted to Ontario from my home province of Nova Scotia. I struggled a lot. To have no control over such a big decision in my life was a hard pill for me to swallow. Roots and stability have always been top priorities in my life. I wanted that one constant—a part of my life that didn't change. People may come and go, but I knew where my home was. Turns out, my soul had a lesson in store. I was now in a new city, and I knew no one. At the time, we had two children, and for the first time, they were both in school. I was left to my own devices, and I honestly didn't know what to do with myself. I didn't have any idea who I was outside of being a wife and mom of two. I had ample time to think about it, but I didn't want any part of it.

ALL I WANTED WAS TO HAVE ANOTHER BABY IN MY ARMS.

We got pregnant straight away, and I was overjoyed! I had put my request out into the Universe and had received it. I spent my days daydreaming about who this little one would be. My intuition has *always* been finely tuned, and I often had a sense when something was going to happen. In my previous pregnancies, I had dreamt of my baby's gender, their looks, and their names. I expected to have that same deep connection with this baby. I did not, and it unnerved me. It made me feel very anxious. Something didn't feel right, but how do you go to your GP and say, "Hey, I'm not dreaming of my baby. I think something is wrong?" I decided to wait. I told myself I was being crazy.

EVERYTHING WOULD BE JUST FINE.

A few weeks later, I flew back to Nova Scotia because my dad was having surgery. I remember sitting in the hospital waiting room wondering what my kids were doing at that time. Being so far away from them was extremely difficult for me, and I was worried sick about my dad. In the back of my mind, this sense of unease kept bouncing around. Something was wrong. I got up to use the bathroom and saw the blood seeping through my jeans.

I WAS LOSING MY MUCH LONGED-FOR BABY.

I began bleeding heavily as soon as I got home from the airport. I spent days in the bathtub, staring off into space, feeling numb and raw. A blighted ovum. That's what the obstetrician called it. One of the most common reasons for miscarriage. However, I was told my case was unusual because it usually happens very early on in pregnancy. I was fourteen weeks, and only days away from announcing our pregnancy to the world. My belly had started to grow. I felt constant nausea. I had acne. My hair was greasy. What happened? What did I do wrong? How could I have felt pregnant for fourteen weeks, yet my baby had likely passed away weeks prior? *I had let my guard down and failed to protect my child.* "The Dragon" was back and these were her words.

In the weeks and months that followed, I became consumed by the thought of conceiving again. I felt so hallowed out, and I needed to feel whole again. Months went by. Negative pregnancy tests piled up in the trash can. After a year of trying, I decided I needed to get real with myself. It wasn't going to happen. I looked The Dragon in the face, and with my voice shaking, I told her that it wasn't my fault, and she wasn't going to make me feel as if it were. It just wasn't in the cards, and I was going to be okay. I tried hard to convince myself of this truth. My kids were growing up, and it was time I gave myself permission to get reacquainted with myself—whoever the heck that was! I found a part-time job. I took up biking. I started running again. I volunteered at our local military family resource centre and at my children's school. I discovered that I actually enjoyed being alone, in my own company. I gradually began to feel full again.

"I'M PREGNANT."

I felt like laughing out loud as I told my husband. What kind of crazy joke was the Universe playing? I think his exact words were "Well, this is unexpected." We were both in shock but good shock. We looked at each other knowingly, hopefully. We'd been here before.

We were old pros.

We decided that since we'd been given this unexpected gift, we'd like the baby's gender to be a surprise. I gave my intuition instructions: "I don't want to know this time. I want a surprise." My intuition listened. I had no gut feelings about the baby, which was unnerving! I experienced a lot of cramping in the second trimester, and I remember calling my midwife in a panic, so fearful that I was losing another baby. On the way to her office, two big rainbows appeared in the sky after a sudden downpour. Peace washed over me in that moment. *We'd be just fine.* The Universe was reminding me to surrender and trust.

My pregnancy was a breeze up until the last month. I experienced constant prodromal labour. I began to lose trust in my body. Is this it? No? Repeat daily. My midwife suggested that I needed to make a plan and then release my own need to control the outcome. The next day, our baby boy was born at home surrounded by his adoring parents and siblings. The missing piece of our puzzle had been found.

I often reflect on that initial appointment with my GP that revealed my fear of abandonment. That fear of abandonment has led me to a pattern of losing myself in other people, be it a friend, a romantic partner, or my child. I've realized that I never felt like a whole person. Perhaps you've felt like that too. We think everyone has it all figured out, but everyone has their own struggles. No one really knows what they are doing. We are all figuring it out as we go.

In January 2018, I lost my dad unexpectedly. Losing my dad felt like losing a part of myself.

THE UNIVERSE TOOK SOMEONE FROM ME AGAIN, AND I COULDN'T DO A DAMN THING ABOUT IT.

I grieved over all the words left unsaid and all the experiences stolen from us. To my surprise, his passing ended up being the catalyst for rediscovering myself. In my grief, I saw myself from a new perspective. The parts of me that I tried to hide were the parts that were most important for me to accept and to heal. They were the very things I came here to share with the world.

We often view anxiety through a lens of fear. It can make us feel like we need to run away, like it's the enemy. Looking back, I see that I wasn't meant to run *away* from anything.

I WAS MEANT TO RUN *TOWARD* SOMETHING, AND THAT SOMETHING WAS *MYSELF*.

You see, "The Dragon" doesn't always show up to tear us down. Sometimes she shows up, holds a mirror up to our faces and says, "Heal this. Work on this. This is Hard but you are Strong." Sometimes we have to lose ourselves in order to find ourselves. Sometimes we break so we can put ourselves back together.

Kintsugi is the Japanese art of gluing broken pottery back together with gold. Each piece is important. Each flaw or scar is beautiful and purposeful. As a whole, the piece is stronger and more resilient than it was before it broke. I think we are all like this too. *Broken, bruised, strong, loving, courageous, fire-breathing dragon slayers.*

Learning that "The Dragon" wasn't my enemy but a friend of sorts has helped me grow exponentially. "The Dragon," for me, is equal parts anxiety and intuition, and they can be easily confused. Her anxious side is meant to protect you. But she can be reactive and overzealous, and she can go too far. She's got her foot planted firmly on the brake. That part of her wants you to STOP or hold back. Her intuitive side is there to guide you. Your personal GPS. This part of her has a heavy foot on the gas and wants you to experience everything you came here to see/feel/do/know/explore. She wants you to GO! The key, I've discovered, is to learn to navigate when it's time to pump the brakes and when it's time to completely floor it.

I don't have to live in fear of "The Dragon" anymore.

She's not my Master.

I am Hers.

Amy Brookes

Amy Brookes was an introverted and quiet child who picked up her first book at age four and fell in love. Books have always been her thing, and she dreamt of being an author when she "grew up." Becoming a published author by sharing this story is a dream come true. As a highly sensitive person and empath, Amy was often prone to feelings of overwhelm by taking on the emotions and energy of others from a very young age, leading her to a feeling of disconnection—a lack of confidence, connection, and belief in herself.

After the sudden passing of her dad, Amy experienced a spiritual awakening and was able to reconnect to who she came here to be. She realized that her sensitivity was actually her superpower.

As a down-to-earth and heart-centred intuitive, and after decades of experiencing the wonders of the Universe for herself, Amy took the leap and launched her spiritual business, Medium Amy Brookes, in early 2019.

Armed with a diploma in office management, a bachelor's degree in psychology, years of work experience in human resources and community health, and more than a decade of holding down the fort for her busy family, Amy's approach to her work and life in general is based on compassion and driven by connection.

Amy is honest and transparent about all her "messy" parts. Being real with her community and global client base is extremely important to her. Her philosophy is that Sharing leads to Trust. Trust leads to Connection. Connection leads to Inspiration, Motivation, and Healing. No one has it all figured out, but none of us are on our own in our struggles. By sharing her own personal struggles, Amy hopes others will feel safe to do the same. Let's start sharing our "messy" parts! That's where the magic happens.

"Authentic, heart of gold, ethical, messenger between the realms, bursting with compassion, and filled with integrity" are some ways in which Amy's community and clients have described her.

We all have a *Why*: The feeling that drives you. The things that fuel you. Your very reason for being. Amy stepped into her Why and her life's purpose—helping others with their grief and healing process by giving them the tools to do so and empowering them to live their best lives. Serving others with her intuitive gifts, Amy offers mediumship and intuitive guidance sessions 1:1 and in groups and is currently working on a mentorship course.

Amy lives in Kingston, Ontario, with her handsome man in uniform and their three sensitive and spirited children. When she is not caring for her family, working with her clients, and slaying dragons, she can be found recording her podcast, buying too many books, and daydreaming about the day she moves to her forever home by the ocean in Nova Scotia.

Scott—*The first, my last, my everything. Home is wherever I'm with you!*

To my children—*I wrote this for you. You are warriors. Thank you for choosing me as your mom.*

Nanny—*You'll always be my greatest role model. I love you more than I can say.*

Mom—*Thank you for teaching me I could be both sensitive and strong.*

To My Men in Spirit: Dad, John, Poppy and baby Henry—*Thank you for showing me the way back to myself. Until we meet again . . .*

To my fellow Anxiety Warriors—*You came to this world with an endless amount of empathy and feeling because you are a powerful force with which to be reckoned. Your sensitivity is your superpower. You are a gift to the world. Never stop fighting.*

My darling girl, when are you going to realize that being "normal" is not necessarily a virtue? It sometimes rather denotes a lack of courage.

~Aunt Frances, Practical Magic[1]

I am not afraid . . . I was born to do this.

~Joan of Arc[2]

She Is

Capable

CHAPTER 7

I DECIDE WHAT I AM CAPABLE OF

Sara Glendenning

As I sit here about to write this chapter, I am transformed back to my four-year-old self. I am sitting at a desk, pencil in hand, staring down at the paper. I can't read yet; my teacher is reading out the instructions to the class. Write out the alphabet. Okay, I think I can do this. I start to write. ∀ b ɔ P. "Oh, no," I think, I don't know what is next, I can't do this. My stomach is starting to hurt, and I think I am going to be sick. My parents are going to be upset; I don't want to upset them. My palms begin to sweat; I don't want to do this anymore. I want to hide, run away. I start looking around the room. Careful, don't get caught. I look up. There they are, the answers on the wall. Relief. I take a deep breath as I start to copy them down. This moment is my first memory of school. It is a memory that is the beginning of many memories that would define my life for more than three decades.

You see, at four years old, I felt the shame of not knowing something that I was expected to know. I recognized that I did not know the answers. I had feelings of not being capable, and I feared disappointing my parents. I wanted them to be proud of me. As I made my way through my early elementary school years, I did my best to hide what I did not know. I avoided being called on by teachers. I worked hard and did my best, eager to learn, but I also recognized that I was making mistakes. Going into grade three, I struggled with letter and word recognition. I was still unable to write simple words or recognize letters consistently. No matter how hard I worked, I continued to make mistakes. I felt alone and incapable. Regardless of my attempts at doing my best, my teachers recognized that I was struggling. I was placed in the Identified Student or Special-Needs Education Program and began to receive one-on-one help in the hopes of reaching the reading level of my peers.

After being diagnosed with Visual Perceptual Deficit, a type of learning disability, I started the "Vision Improvement Program," in which I completed different brain training exercises to assist me in letter recognition. I loathed these exercises. I remember sitting at the desk, wanting to run and hide. I was frustrated with learning, as I continually struggled and felt alone. No matter how hard I worked, I was left feeling incapable of answering simple questions, things my peers had learned years before. Within this program, I was introduced to the "I can" box. When I voiced feelings of being incapable, of not being enough, or said "I can't," I was not allowed to continue an activity until I proudly stated "I can" into the box. Gosh, I hated that box. I remember sessions when the box never left the table because I could not get beyond the mindset that I was struggling with the activity, and there were sessions when I would refuse to speak into the box. But this box, although simple, forced me to change my thoughts. It forced me to believe that I am capable of more than what I feel in the moment. I can do hard things. I am capable.

Throughout the program, I was encouraged and guided to believe in my capabilities, but outside of it, I continued to struggle with schoolwork. I felt alone and different than my peers. For grade three, I was placed in a smaller class that allowed more one-on-one education with the teacher and a specialized learning plan. Throughout the year, I joined a regular classroom for art class, but it was not something I looked forward to. I felt out of place and lonely. I was embarrassed about being different. I can still remember the feeling I had in my stomach as I walked from my classroom to the portable. It felt full of knots, and like I was going to be sick. I felt gross and ashamed, judged and alone. I do not remember being bullied in school for being different. These feelings came from within me—a longing to be like everyone else. Feeling out of place with my peers became the norm for me; I was different and no longer had things in common with them. Even when surrounded by my peers, I felt socially isolated, alone in a battle against myself.

My favourite word growing up was *why*. I wanted to know the ways of the world and why things were the way they were. Similarly, I wanted to know why I was placed in a smaller class. I was told that my brain was missing a connection and that I had to work extra hard to teach my brain what to do. All I heard was that I was different. That there was something wrong with me. No one could *see* how I was different, but I could *feel* it. I assumed that what I struggled with came easily to everyone else. No one around me seemed to have difficulty with school the way I did. These thoughts and feelings further isolated me in a world where I already felt alone. I became less social, sticking close to those around me and wanting to hide how I was different. I was terrified of being as different or weird on the outside as I felt on the inside. If I did not allow people to get to know me and only shared what looked and felt the same as others, they would not know my secret.

My mom picked me up on the last day of school, which was a special treat because we only lived a short walking distance away. The final bell rang, and we all ran outside, excited for the adventures summer would bring. When I got into the car, I knew something was wrong. I ripped open my report card to see how I had done. The news that followed I never expected. I would not be moving onto grade four with my friends the following year. I was going to have to do grade three again, this time in the regular stream. I felt like I was lost in a bad dream; I was confused. I had done all that was asked of me. I could read and spell, and school was finally making sense. I felt capable, and I was no longer struggling as much. It was simple; my learning plan over the previous year meant that I did not complete all the grade three requirements. I had not participated in science, geography, history, or art. I was now behind in other topics. I believed that I could—and I did—work really damn hard. But it was clear that no matter how hard I worked, I still was not enough.

Regardless of having many incredible teachers along the way, the system did not have the time or resources to support me on its own. I was told that I wouldn't, couldn't, and was not capable. The prognosis: I would not graduate from high school. I would not become anything. The school board planned to support me as much as possible, but post-secondary education was an unrealistic expectation that I would not meet. These statements and judgments came from provincial data and standardized tests and were based on the results of the children who had come before me. My future was predicted before I was given a chance to prove myself or show the world what I was capable of achieving.

After the news was a period of shock, followed by years of anger toward my mom. My dad had been an equal participant in the decision to hold me back, but my mom received the brunt of my anger and resentment. I was alone and different, even from my family. I was a failure. Before, I had been alone among my peers, but I had my family on my side. But now it was clear that they did not believe in me either. I was truly alone, which was a story I created from the anger and hurt that I felt, a story I would carry for many, many years and which could not have been further from the truth. From that point forward, I felt that the only person who believed in me was *me*. At that age, I was unable to see the bigger picture. I did not understand how this defining moment of failing grade three would catapult me forward to do incredible things otherwise not possible. My relationship with my mom became defined by blame—I blamed her for doing it TO me. I grieved the life I thought I was supposed to have, and I relived the grief every year when my best friend and I talked about how maybe the next year we would be in the split class. I held onto hope that I could return in some way to where I was "supposed" to be. I created expectations for outcomes that were followed by disappointment and frustration that I was different and alone, that I was not worthy of being in classes with my friends. I projected these feelings onto my mom for years because it was her fault. She was responsible for holding me back from the life I was entitled to lead. If only she had let me continue on the way it was supposed to go, things would have been better, easier.

Unworthy, alone, and defeated—all words that defined my education from a young age. All words that I worked hard to overcome. Proving the school system wrong became the purpose that propelled me through grade school. It was my *why*, my need to not be or feel different. In eighth grade I participated in class without the direct support of special education (SPED). It was still available to me as needed, but I was participating in the regular stream. I felt capable. School was still difficult at times, and I had to work hard, but I was proud of myself. I felt like I fit in. I felt normal. I was approached by my teacher near the end of the year. I had done it—I was on track to receive the honour's award. But the conversation that followed further ingrained my belief that I was unworthy. The school leaders had decided that I was not deserving of the award that year, as I was still considered to be a part of the SPED program. I was assisted, thus not equal, so not deserving of the award, regardless of the fact I had participated in the regular stream just like my peers. I felt the words as my teacher spoke. They were a punch to my stomach and tears welled up behind my eyes. I was angry, hurt, and frustrated, and I questioned why I even tried, why I worked so damn hard. The system would win. No matter how hard I worked, I would never be equal; I would never become more, just as they had been telling me all along. To my surprise on graduation day, I received the award, but the damage had been done. My worth again taken.

Near the end of high school, I began drinking alcohol. It started as a means to fit in with my peers. What I quickly learned was that when I drank, everything was okay, and I had a false sense of freedom from the expectations of being an equal to those around me.

I no longer felt lonely. When I was intoxicated, I felt important. I felt capable and worthy of anything I put my mind to. The world weighed less, and I was free. After a few years of heading in no specific direction, my days spent working multiple minimum-wage jobs and nights filled with the consumption of alcohol—essentially living a life without a purpose and just passing the time—I knew that I could not continue on the road I was travelling. I started the journey to find a path for my life through therapy. It helped, and I slowly stopped drinking as I began to have faith in myself. I started to believe in my core that I was capable and worthy, regardless of the events of my childhood. While in therapy, I frequently voiced the anger and resentment I carried toward my mom for the decision she had made when I was a child. I blamed her for making my life hard, for making the decision to hold me back from the life that I was supposed to live. But I learned in therapy that blame and fear were holding me back. I believed that I had released it, as I found the courage to move forward, but little did I know that this round of therapy was only brushing the surface of what was holding me back.

I took a chance and applied to a nursing degree program. I was terrified of failing again, of giving it my best and it not being enough. Throughout public school I had been surrounded by support. When things got hard, I had a safety net of people who would provide me with the support I needed and catch me before I fell. Post-secondary schools do provide resources to students with disabilities. There were programs I could utilize, but I really did not want to use them. I desperately wanted to be normal. I did not want my professors to know my story. I wanted to be marked equally to my peers, not due to a preconception of what I was capable of achieving. But I was also terrified that when marked on an equal level and not knowing my weakness, I would not be enough, that I would truly be what the school had said I was all along. I also wanted my peers to view me as equal and not lesser than. I was so tired of being the girl who was a failure. And I was most afraid that if I failed, I would not reach what others thought was my highest potential, and I would disappoint them.

I found the courage to believe I was capable. I was accepted to the nursing degree program. Oh, the excitement! I finally felt like I had a purpose. After the first year, I felt aligned. I was shocked by my marks; they provided the external validation that I craved to prove to myself that I was capable. And while assisting nurses in the field, I started to believe that I had what it took to be a nurse.

Well into second year, the internal trust I had in my capabilities became challenged. My grades were slipping, and I wanted to quit. I was pulled into the feelings and emotions of my childhood, and I had fear that I truly was not capable. I became overwhelmed by the expectations of the program, my own expectations, and the perceived expectations of others, all in combination with the demands of everyday life. I felt alone and unsupported and like I had to do it all on my own. For me, accepting help was a sign of weakness. All that I wanted was to prove that I was capable, which meant that I was able to manage and handle school, work, and the pressures of adult life without receiving the help of others. And when things got hard, I did not reach out for help. I dug deep and attempted to keep going. I was not sleeping, I stopped eating, I started hallucinating, and I was unable to focus until I had an unexpected visit from my mom. On her arrival it was clear that I was not managing, that I was not okay, and that I needed help I wasn't willing to ask for. I was forced to accept this help, as bags were packed and I was transported home after a stop at our local emergency department. I was horrified. I had proven to the world again that I was not capable, that I was weak. I was embarrassed to be there, requiring help. I received a prescription to treat anxiety and depression, and we were on our way to my childhood home. There, I took pills that treated the immediate side effects of the panic attack that lasted three long weeks. I soon realized, however, that the medication was only masking the surface of the deeper issues I was not yet ready to face.

When I think back to that time, I remember feeling as though I was living in an out-of-body experience. I wanted to quit the program. I no longer believed in myself, and I felt that I was not capable of completing it. My fear of failing was more than my belief that I was not capable. Not completing the program was no different than repeating a grade. But I had been a disappointment before, and I did not want to be one again. This thought propelled me forward, and I continued in the program. Through this experience I learned that I need to be open to accepting help when offered or to ask for help when I am struggling. Asking for help remains a challenge and is not something I do easily, but I do know now that it is NOT a sign of weakness; it IS a sign of strength.

It was time to celebrate! The goal, the expectation was met. I DID it. I achieved what others said was an impossible goal for me. I completed an honour's degree, and I am a registered nurse. But I did not want to celebrate the success. I had completed the program out of a need to prove others wrong. I proved that I was not a failure and that I can do hard things, but I still felt alone and unworthy of celebrating. Instead, I focused on what was next: find a job, eliminate my school debt, and see what the future held for me. If I stayed focused, then I could ignore the fear that I may not like what I saw when I looked in the mirror—a scared, sad, tired little girl who was putting on a front to convince the world she believed she could when deep down she was painfully afraid that she couldn't. Deep down, I was afraid that the world would see I was a fraud outside of what I knew. I was terrified that I would not make it as a nurse because I wasn't smart or tough enough, that I would make mistakes and lose my licence. When I looked in the mirror, I saw a girl who could not celebrate or receive positive feedback from others because she was not worthy. She was not worthy of celebration or positive thoughts even from herself.

I was stuck in a cycle of self-talk that was telling me that no one understood what I was going through. I had grown up surrounded by family who believed I was capable of doing anything, and that I would reach my biggest goals. But their beliefs did not mean anything to me because I did not believe them. I heard their words, but how does a girl who could not read or write basic words until well into grade three possibly be capable of doing anything? I truly believed that I was not worthy or able. I have learned that regardless of what others say, if I do not believe in myself, it does not matter what others say or think. Believing in myself, believing that I am capable and worthy of having the life of my dreams has been one of my biggest challenges. I work every day on changing my mindset.

I was once challenged to remove words from my vocabulary, words that were holding me down and from which I was unable to escape. As a result, I have removed those words. I no longer talk about how I am struggling or how things are hard. When you believe you are struggling and that there is no end in sight, you will never stop. The word "struggle" does not encourage you to take action or change your mindset. Instead, I am challenged, I have been challenged throughout my life, and I know that I am capable of overcoming challenges. I can now see the possibility of what this life could hold for me, and I just have to make small changes to overcome one challenge at a time.

It was not until 2020 when I began a journey of self-care that

I realized I still believed the opinions of those in my childhood. I believed that I was not worthy or capable of obtaining the life I craved. Regardless of what I have achieved, I believed that I was not capable of reaching my goals or bringing them to fruition. Not following through with my goals only further proved that I was not capable or worthy of them. This repetitive cycle led to further frustration I had toward myself. Through therapy and mentorship, I began to dig deeper into my past. This process has been difficult and eye opening, but what I have learned about myself has changed my life as I know it. I have forgiven myself for needing more time, and for giving up on my dreams before I gave them a true effort. I have forgiven myself for believing that the life of my dreams is not possible for me, for chasing after where I should be and not embracing where I am, and for not realizing sooner that the opinions of others do not define who I am or what I will become because I am the only one who can decide what I am capable of.

I also realized that I had not truly forgiven my mom. I realized how much anger and resentment I was still carrying toward her. I now know and understand that her decision was not done TO me but FOR me. The resentment I carried changed through this realization to immense gratitude, love, and appreciation. Without this chance, without that hard decision, I would not have the life that I have today. Embracing forgiveness for both my mom and for myself has renewed our relationship in a way I never thought possible for us.

What I learned through forgiveness is that I never failed; I am NOT a failure. I never did anything wrong. I did everything that I was supposed to do, I just needed more time. I am blessed to have the family that I have. Yes, they gave their consent for me to repeat grade three and altered my future. It was a decision I know they did not make lightly. But they also provided me with the support I required to prove the system wrong. They gave me the chance to have a life beyond the dreams of my eight-year-old self—a life that I know I would not have been capable of living without their hard choice. They knew what the system did not—that I was capable of more, and that I would reach my highest potential.

School leaders told me I couldn't, they told me I wouldn't, they told me I was not capable, and they told me I was undeserving. But this girl did. She graduated from high school, she got a nursing degree, she wrote this damn chapter in a published book. She is an author. This moment, it is worth the loneliness, fear, disappointment, hurt, and every tear. After way too many years of being afraid of showing up, of showing her weakness, she is here, and gosh she is finally damn proud of who she has become.

Sara Glendenning

Author, Podcaster, Registered Nurse

At a young age, Sara was told by educators that she would not graduate from high school. After years of hard work, she decided that her success would not end with graduation, and she went on to complete her BScN and began working as a registered nurse.

Hiding from the world became the norm for Sara after she was diagnosed with a learning disability. She lived many years afraid of others' judgment, not showing up as her true self, and always holding parts of herself back. Recently, she realized that she was hiding from herself more than from the world. By working through this fear, she now knows that she is a funny, passionate, adventurous, intuitive, and lovable woman when she allows her true self to shine. Sara now genuinely believes she can live the life of her dreams; she knows that it was her own beliefs that were holding her back. This realization has changed Sara's life. She has made it her mission to inspire others to overcome the fear of others' judgment, and mostly their own. She encourages others to ultimately show up as their true selves, to be proud of who they are, and to live the life of their dreams.

When Sara is not working as a registered nurse, she is found running the trails of southern Ontario, getting lost in a book, creating tasty treats in the kitchen, or spending time with family and friends.

Mom and Dad, thank you for making the hard decisions. Thank you for not pushing me through the education system when I was not ready. I am grateful for the sacrifices that you have made. Thank you for believing in and supporting me, even when I made it a challenge. Thank you for pushing me to reach for more when I was happy to settle for less. I am who I am today because of the strength you gave me.

Denise and Peter, thank you for your continued support and for inspiring my love of reading. Thank you for being my personal editors and my sounding board and for giving me a second place to call home. Thank you for always supporting my crazy dreams and helping me bring them to life, and thank you for having my back and for all the sacrifices you made for me over the years.

To the teachers and support staff who believed in me, challenged me, and sometimes scared me, thank you!

Finally, to the human that has been told that you are not capable of bringing your wild, beautiful dreams to life: know that the only person that can decide what you are capable of is you. Believe in yourself and know that no matter what you choose, you are worthy of bringing your dreams to life.

She Is

Brave

CHAPTER 8

UNTITLED PUNK SONG

Melanie Matthews

Storytelling is important. Through telling stories, we can connect and empathize with one another. We learn and grow and support each other through our stories and experiences. However, stories can also be used to alienate or "one up" others. To keep them at a distance. To shock or even to scare them. I've always used stories as a way to get a reaction from the person I'm talking to. And not just any reaction. No, I want that open-mouthed, wide-eyed, shocked expression that leaves the person unable to respond except by saying, "Oh, my god, I can't believe that happened." Because if I couldn't relate to the positive, wholesome, happy stories that others have, well, I'd may as well just push them as far away from me as I can get them. It's isolating, but it feels safer than opening up to other people and letting them really see me.

It took a lot for me to reach a point where I'm able to share my story from a position of connecting with others. I no longer want to shock or scare people into staying away. I've learned to trust again and to be vulnerable. I want to share. It took more than ten years of education, therapy, and amazing friends who were open enough to tell me their stories for me to feel as though I've grown from my experiences enough to be able to relate to others again.

This is my story.

I met *him* when I was fourteen, right at the beginning of high school. He was dating my best friend, and I was dating his best friend. This situation lasted for about two weeks and then we literally traded partners, which may seem strange, but we lived in a small town of about 11,000 people with only one high school. The chances of dating someone's ex were pretty high considering there just weren't that many people available. Our relationship progressed in the expected way for a teenage relationship. There was a lot of nervous hand holding and hanging out during lunch breaks at school. It was before cellphones were something every teenager had, so I spent a lot of time sitting on top of my dresser talking to him on my black corded phone until my parents forced me to do homework instead. There were no red flags, no big issues. Not yet, anyway. My mother always said she didn't like him much, something that made me angry, but a mother's intuition is a powerful thing. I just didn't believe it yet. Eventually, we broke up anyway. However, this relationship wouldn't be over for good.

During that time, I also experimented with drugs and alcohol like a lot of teenagers do. My use started small. I tried smoking weed with my best friend, and we found that we really liked it. At first it wasn't a big deal; we just smoked a bit after school or on the weekends. But then we started getting high during lunch breaks at school. Then before first period. Soon, we started skipping classes entirely. It wasn't a big deal until suddenly, it was. By the time we were fifteen, we were smoking weed nearly every day and drinking excessively. I think I need to clarify what "excessively" means because when it comes to alcohol, I think that it means something different to every person. Between the two of us, we could knock off at least a 26er of vodka and smoke some weed on top of it. We were both around a hundred pounds and didn't really eat regularly. We weren't just getting tipsy and giggly, we were getting blackout wasted and ended up in a lot of dangerous situations because of how drunk we were.

Things started to go really downhill after I turned sixteen. My best friend and I still hung out, smoking weed and drinking, but now we were also stealing and breaking into places. My parents had always been strict, and my rebellion only inspired more restrictions. My curfew was 4:00 p.m. I had to be home to do my chores, eat dinner, and work my shift as a cashier at the grocery store across the street. I would sometimes be allowed to go out again after dinner if I didn't have to work, but only until 10:00 p.m. None of my friends had such an early curfew, especially on weekends. I felt alone and left out. Everyone would come to school the next day, laughing about what had happened the night before, while I had been in bed fuming about being left behind by my friends. It got to the point where my friends stopped even asking me to hang out, to go to birthday parties, or to spend time with them because they knew my parents' answer would be no. Those restrictions meant the death of my social life, something I couldn't tolerate. I started staying at other friends' houses more because they didn't have such strict parents. That way, I could go wherever I wanted, whenever I wanted. And in a small town, that usually meant the local high school or some park to drink or smoke weed since there was no movie theatre or mall. We didn't even have a Walmart. So, we made our own fun doing stupid, dangerous things like climbing onto the school roof or going to parties with older guys we didn't know.

During the winter after I turned sixteen, I left home. There were a lot of fights and awful events that all culminated in me throwing my belongings into a couple black duffel bags and trash bags, then telling my parents, "I'm leaving now and I'm not coming back." I left, and I didn't go back. And with that action of leaving home, I'd gone from being a straight-A student with a promising athletic future to a runaway teen. Turns out, there weren't many places that a sixteen-year-old could afford to rent while working part time at the grocery store, so I ended up on the street. Since I lived in such a small town, there weren't any homeless shelters or group homes to go to either. I was on my own to figure out where to stay. I ended up squatting in a townhouse in a low-income housing complex for about two months. If you just walk into a home and no one tells you to leave right away, it's actually surprisingly hard for the owner or the authorities to make you move out. Once teachers and other adults in my life realized what was happening, instead of offering help, a chorus of voices said, "You've really screwed up" and "You're never even going to graduate high school." I was labelled "at risk" and removed from extracurricular activities and specialized university prep courses. No one believed in me, so I stopped believing in myself. I defined myself by those words and used them as a justification for every terrible decision I made next. Why bother ever being sober? Why should I do homework? Why not skip every class and get kicked out of high school? Who was going to say no to that now that I'm just an at-risk runaway?

I wasn't alone, though. *He* was there too, since he left his parents' home a few months before I did. I started dating him again, but it was different this time. We were different. We weren't naïve fourteen-year-old kids anymore. Don't get me wrong, we were definitely still kids, but we had lost the innocent quality we had had before and now there were some serious red flags. We were angry, drunk, and living together, which is not a recipe for a healthy relationship at any age, but it is particularly volatile for a couple of teenagers. I was a rebound for him after a particularly bad breakup, and he was a life raft for me to cling to when I had no idea what I was doing on my own. I may not have liked my parents' rules, but I was completely unprepared to make my own. He took control over my life, and I let him because it was far easier than trying to figure things out on my own. He made the decisions for every aspect of my life. He chose where we would live, what we ate for dinner, where I was allowed to work, and who our friends would be. He also decided what drugs we would use and how we would use them. It was a relief to have him take control. I was used to being told what to do by my parents, so it was more comfortable for me to submit to his demands. I was scared to think for myself, and there were bigger things happening in our small town that I was not capable of dealing with on my own.

Do you remember the start of the opioid epidemic in Ontario? The moment when Oxycontin entered the scene, touted as a non-addictive painkiller? The answer to the prayers of many looking for relief without risk. I remember. I remember because I was tricked by him into using Oxy for the first time. I didn't mean to do it. Honestly, I was afraid of Oxy because I had started to see how badly it was affecting some of my friends. They didn't look healthy anymore, and some had been arrested on drug and assault charges. I thought he was giving me something else, and I trusted him to not give me anything that would hurt me. Turns out that Oxy is, in fact, addictive, which I found out fast. I was furious at him for tricking me into using Oxy, but I used it again the very next day. Why? Something in my brain decided that I needed it. Soon,

I wasn't getting sick from using, I was getting sick when I didn't use. Swallow, snort, and smoke—I did everything except shoot them. I can still remember the taste of the smoke, and I still have holes in my nose from chemical burns. The need was so intense that it consumed my thoughts and took away everything else in my life that had previously been important. No more school. No more sports. No more family. Not only was I an at-risk runaway, I was a drug addict.

The thing about being addicted to drugs is that you become much easier to manipulate. I think back now and wonder whether I would have stayed if he hadn't been supplying my drugs. Would I have stayed if he didn't have that power over me? Regardless, I did stay, and it was awful. I made a lot of excuses for him and tried to explain away his behaviour. "He was stressed. I was annoying him. He was high." It didn't help that a lot of our friends knew how toxic our relationship was but did nothing to intervene. To me, that was more confirmation that I should just endure it to prove how committed I was to the relationship. I really thought that if I could just do better, then the relationship would improve. One day, out of the blue, he decided that we were no longer going to use drugs, and we were going to move out of our small town into a bigger city. I still have no idea what motivated this change, but I went along with it. I quit Oxy and moved with him. With a bit of family support, we were able to get into a nice, two-bedroom apartment that was fully renovated with deep green carpets. I remember those carpets because I thought they were absolutely beautiful and that this time around I could keep them clean and perfect so we could have a comfortable place to live. It would be a fresh start.

Even though we weren't using anymore, our relationship worsened. Despite each promise that he would change, there was always another incident even worse than the last. Normally, this would be the time that I would tell you exactly what happened. All the horrific facts without sparing a single detail because I wouldn't want you to get too close to me. You couldn't possibly empathize with what happened, so I'd rather see your shocked face and wide eyes. I want to hear you say, "Oh, my god, I can't believe that happened." But I've decided not to. Maybe you can empathize after all. You've probably gone through your own challenges, and even if they aren't the same as mine, you can understand what it's like when life gets hard and everything feels hopeless. So, I won't shock you and try to drive you away. I want to tell you my story in a way that feels like connection. All you need to know is that it got about as bad as it can get, but finally, he left. He left me alone without any friends or family in a city I didn't know and with an apartment I couldn't possibly pay for on my own. I was completely devastated. Rejected. At the time, it didn't feel liberating or like a success to have that relationship end. Really, it felt like a huge loss, and I grieved that relationship despite all the awful things he had done to me.

In terms of events, I don't actually remember what happened for the next six months or so after the breakup. I was in a fog, just drifting. I had no short-term memory and often couldn't remember what had happened even just the day before. Can you imagine how embarrassing it is to meet someone and then forget their name and face just the next day? I withdrew from all social situations. I stopped talking to even my old friends. Like I said, I don't actually remember that happening, but that's what I was told when I finally came back to reality. When I finally came back, I also found that I had lost around fifteen pounds, which left me with my five-foot, four-inch frame weighing only about ninety pounds. I guess when you have no short-term memory, it's also hard to remember to eat.

Things didn't get better for me immediately after the relationship ended. First, I hit an all-time low, just repeating the same day over and over and over again. I worked my shift, 3:30 to 11:30 p.m., then dragged myself back to my apartment in my uniform that smelled of burned coffee that I rarely ever changed out of. I didn't even bother to bring my bike because what would I be rushing back for? Might as well walk and fill my day with something. One day I was shuffling along with my ugly regulation black work shoes with my head down, shoulders slumped, hair spilling over my face, then completely out of nowhere, I stopped. I still can't pinpoint what exactly happened in the moment, but all of a sudden, I was angry. And not just angry, but absolutely pissed off! All I could think was "How dare he? How dare he make me feel like this?"

At that moment, I made a decision. I decided that I was never going to let someone make me feel worthless and hopeless ever again. I would not let him define how I would live my life anymore. I raised my head, straightened my shoulders, and started walking with purpose.

Of course, nothing actually changed right away. I won't pretend that it was as simple as that to turn my entire life around. It was still an effort every day to hold my head up and keep moving forward. But I did it. I re-enrolled in high school after missing most of my grade 11 year, and I did absolutely terribly in every single one of my classes because I still had to work and struggle to get by. I managed to stay off the Oxy with intense willpower plus the fact that I didn't live in the same town as the dealers I knew, so I couldn't find the drugs even when my conviction wavered. I also didn't really have any goals I was working toward. I figured I'd keep my nose clean, graduate high school, then maybe become a manager at Tim Hortons. Nothing wrong with that, but I had never been particularly good at customer service and was eventually fired, so that was never going to work out. I still saw myself as an at-risk teenage drug addict. An abused girl not capable of thinking for myself. Worthless. But then, someone noticed me. She was a guidance counsellor at my high school who was just doing her job by disciplining me, a student who had way too many absences. At that point, I was absent more than I was in class without giving any excuses or explanations to any of my teachers, so naturally, it was time for someone to intervene and give me detention or something. She confronted me, and when I said I was absent because I had to work, she responded, "Well, what's more important? Your education or working your part-time job?" I remember the shocked look on her face when I said, "My job." I explained that I would be homeless for the second time in my life if I didn't make enough money to pay rent. Instead of giving me detention or telling me I was too "at risk" to be welcome at school, she gave me granola bars, vouchers to get free food at the cafeteria, and some bus tickets. Not only that, she checked in with me often. Even more importantly, she intervened with all my teachers to make sure they didn't fail me for being absent too often.

When it became clear that I would be able to graduate, the guidance counsellor did one more thing for me. She told me I should go to college. I didn't know anything about college or how to apply because I hadn't intended on continuing my education. I'm pretty sure there were at least a couple of days when that topic was covered in my classes, and I'm 100 percent sure I didn't go to class those days. So, she sat down with me in the computer lab and helped me apply. She even picked my program for me: the Child and Youth Worker program. She said she thought in a couple of years I would be great at helping kids who were like me. She said that people who have experienced hard things in their life were the best people to help others. That moment was the first time I felt like someone believed in me. I had so internalized the opinions of everyone who doubted me when I first left my parents' home that I hadn't even considered that I had something valuable to offer the world. My guidance counsellor could see something different in me even though I still saw myself as undeserving of a rewarding future because of who I was. Rejected. Worthless. But after I received my acceptance letter to college, that view of myself began to change and some hope for the future started coming back.

I got lucky. I had a sense of righteous anger at the injustice of being abused and cast aside that drove me to keep trying when it seemed as though the world was working against me. After graduating from high school, I made it through college and then went on to university. I kept that sense of needing to continue to work hard to persevere through seemingly insurmountable odds. The chances of someone who was a homeless teenager addicted to drugs making it through university aren't great. The thing is, those aspects of my identity do not represent all there is to know about me. I beat the odds, and I now have a master's of social work degree and a successful career doing exactly what my guidance counsellor said I would be great at doing. I'm the only one of my friends from high school who has made it through a graduate level of education. I have a partner who loves me, a two-bedroom apartment for us to live in, a cat, and enough money in the bank to not only pay rent every month but to have savings as well. I will not be homeless again. I will not use drugs again. I will certainly not be in a toxic relationship ever again. That's not the case for everyone. There are plenty of people out there right now who are just like me with endless potential but also terribly traumatized, and they're stuck in a seemingly hopeless situation. I know that for a fact because I work with these people now in homeless shelters, in addiction treatment, and in counselling. We often define ourselves by our circumstances and how others see us. But you are not worthless, no matter what anyone else has said to you. Everyone deserves the help and support to get through their challenges in life, regardless of what those challenges are that they face. No matter what you're born into, what mental health or addictions you experience, or what your relationships have been like, your life is not predetermined. It's not your fault if you are being abused or if you have been abused, and it's not fair that you are the one who has to pick yourself up and put the pieces back together, but you can do it. I am living proof that people can defy the odds. While I was homeless and addicted to opioids, that is not the whole sum of my identity. I am a survivor, and I create my own path.

Melanie Matthews

Melanie Matthews is a dedicated social activist, cat parent, and tattoo enthusiast. She is passionate about causes she supports, including advocating for mental health supports. Her life experiences as a trauma survivor have helped shape her into the strong and compassionate person she is today. She lives with a traumatic brain injury that has changed the way she experiences the world, but in no way has it held her back from achieving her goals.

Melanie is a social worker and psychotherapist living and working in Toronto, Ontario. She holds a bachelor's degree in social work as well as a master's degree in social work. Melanie has worked in social services and mental health since 2010 and currently operates a private practice offering individual counselling. Her practice focuses on working with people experiencing depression, anxiety, personality disorders, and distress during life transitions. As well, she works as a consultant for not-for-profits doing research, evaluation, and grant writing. Her current social justice focus is increasing equity and access to resources for Black youth experiencing social isolation. Melanie is a published academic writer with an article in the journal *Social Work Review*, and she has released a number of community reports with not-for-profit organizations.

Outside of her work, Melanie also spends her time spreading knowledge and awareness of social work and mental health treatment through her podcast, the *Social Work Social*. On this podcast she interviews social workers and mental health professionals to share information and stories that will reduce the stigma of receiving mental health treatment. She believes that by working together, we can all contribute to making mental health treatment more accessible to everyone.

She also cross-stitches swear words and argues with her cat, who really needs to get off the counter right now.

She Is

Hopeful

CHAPTER 9

I HAD TO BE BROKEN TO BE WOKEN

Nicole Clark

My journey of self-healing was a rocky road to travel. The healing didn't happen quickly or all at once, yet I can assure you that the reward was worth the effort. From the outside looking in, I had everything. But the truth was that I was unhappy, and my health declined as a result. I was not living my authentic life. Now a single mom, my health is improving, and I feel at peace. My healing journey is not over, yet I am excited for what the future holds, and I know that I am on the right path. It took a lot of time for me to learn that grief is a lesson that I would learn and heal from once I was ready to face it with compassion.

It took experiencing multiple deaths for me to be able to see life. Not all deaths are the same, but they all hurt. The death of a pet, the death of a marriage, the death of a loved one, the death of a relationship, the death of who I was. Death removed all the guards and the walls that I put in place as a child, a teen, and even in my adult years to protect myself. It took death to show me the memory of pain and hurt my body had stored. Every hurt, every trauma, every insult had taken hold somewhere in my body and formed a memory imprint.

Memory is a funny thing. We think we know what it is. Yet memory is your perception of that moment. The associated trauma and suffering have a way of teaching you that memory is more than just what your brain recalls, it is also something your body stores in its own way. The severity of those memories dictated my survival response. That is how I believe we as humans learn how to cope with life.

Can you survive living guarded from life's experiences?

Of course you can. Many people do. I did without even realizing it. Grief broke me down and woke me up. Each death was a different experience and new learning. Life's funny that way; it is the ultimate teacher, and it will keep offering you lessons until you learn. It took living through multiple experiences of grief to show me that I was broken in ways I didn't realize. My story is about what I learned from that pain. It's about me healing by opening myself to feel the pain, the anxiety, and the grief of my life experiences. By opening my heart to feel the grief my body had stored, I survived. It might be hard to believe that somebody could be grateful for so much loss and grief, yet I am grateful. I am truly grateful for those experiences and the lessons my journey has taught me. My hope is that my story might inspire curiosity in you to see that healing from grief means embracing it so that you, too, can live mindfully in your own life.

* * *

The broken parts of me were hard to see. I had learned how to hide them behind strength and success. Underneath my success was sadness and disappointment, and below that layer was another deeper one I didn't even realize existed. I discovered I was struggling very deeply with a sense of abandonment. To anybody else it would have looked like anger, but it was a feeling I had learned to bury a very long time ago, and my body remembered it while my mind had forgotten. Once I learned to acknowledge these broken parts, I could see how they held me back from experiencing peace and joy.

Anger, impatience, and intolerance. These feelings and reactions were riddled in everything I did and who I was. They were the by-product of this deep subconscious layer of long buried feeling.

Ultimately, I was uncomfortable in my own skin because I was not living my authentic life. This fact is clear to me in hindsight. Even as I write these words, the picture becomes slowly clearer. Before my healing journey began, I was just angry and impatient. I spent my days without happiness, joy, or laughter. I pushed through each experience in this joyless state. I simply wanted to get things done or to tick a box. I did not slow down or enjoy any of the moments. I was successful, and many people might say I was living a life of privilege. Yet my reality was one of mere survival. I was just trying to get to the next step in life, barreling through life trading happiness for accomplishment.

When I was twelve years old, my brother, who was in the Navy, came home for a visit. I was so excited to see him and to hear about his journey around the world. I was counting the months, days, weeks, and minutes until the moment he arrived. The day he came home, I was so excited. I put on a pretty dress, tied ribbons in my hair, and waited patiently. He arrived with a suitcase of gifts he gathered along his travels. A koala bear and a boomerang from Australia, a jade necklace and earrings from the Orient, sheep rugs from New Zealand.

I was excited to see and spend time with my older brother. Looking back on that time now, my memory is less about the gifts, which I kept but put in a box out of sight, and more about what happened in the kitchen. It is one of my last memories of my brother. Once he had time to greet everybody and things settled down, we all went to the kitchen. He sat at the kitchen table with my other brother. All I wanted was a seat at the table. His return was supposed to be a highlight for me, and all I wanted was a hug, a kiss, and some time with him. Yet in the kitchen at that table, nobody made any room for me to join the family reunion.

I was pushed away. "Get lost, Nikki, go away, Nikki" I was told. It was a slap in the face I wasn't expecting. The dismissal took me by surprise, and it hurt. It was a big stab to my heart. I left the kitchen and went sobbing to my room. I felt like this dismissal was the common theme of my childhood. It was the way I grew up, and this response became a very familiar one for me. I still clearly and vividly remember feeling the sadness and disappointment of not being seen or heard. I felt alone and unwanted.

I remember the summer of 1999 well. I was happy, carefree, and broke. I was working as a server and had no worries. I had spent that summer living on a sailboat and sailing around Granville Island, Vancouver. It was one of the best summers of my life. In 2014 memories of that summer called me back to sailing. I remembered being at my happiest when I was on the water.

It's a strange thing to think that we can become so unhappy that even laughter becomes distant and foreign, like something you only read about. This realization came to me one hot sunny day out on the boat. It was me, the instructor, the sun and the water, and I laughed. Laughter had become so foreign to me that I instantly felt uncomfortable with its strangeness. It was a split second. It was a wake-up call for me. I remember thinking, "Hey, you! I remember you. You're fun, where have you been?"

In that brief moment of laughter, I realized that I had made myself small over the years. I had learned to accommodate others, to make other people happy and hide from the pain in my heart. The pain of being in a loveless marriage, the pain of feeling unappreciated, the pain of coming from a dysfunctional family, the pain of losing my sister, the pain of losing myself in the grief I felt.

Death's brother, Grief, is what enables us and disables us through life. Grief can be all-consuming, devastating, debilitating, insurmountable, and un-survivable. At its worst, it takes over and you are merely existing as time passes by. The world continues around you without a care for the pain you are suffering. In grief, we lose a part of ourselves, and when we come out of grief, we are never the same person. It has changed us.

In these difficult moments we make choices that shape our future selves in unpredictable and even unconscious ways. We are faced with questions, and the choices we make determine our outcome. The questions can be simple: Can I get out of bed? Can I make it to the mailbox without completely breaking down in tears? In answering these seemingly mundane questions, we make choices. When you make a decision, you are choosing life over death. When you choose to act, you are choosing to live. When you're buried in grief, it feels like you are drowning in a sea of sadness. I felt like I was dying.

I was not that close to my father. My parents divorced when I was two, and I grew up feeling like a Ping-Pong ball bouncing between them, each one playing me off the other. On our weekend visits, my dad used me as his lifeline to the family. It became my job to update him on everyone else's life. In fact, it felt like all I did was spend my time talking about other people's lives. My own life felt irrelevant. I hated the questions. I resented them. I dreaded every moment of them.

The impact of these interrogation sessions still resides within me, a memory my body has held onto and one I would much rather release. The trouble is that people ask questions. Most people, of course, are genuine and are simply curious, but each question stirs deep pain in me. Each question is a reminder how small and irrelevant I feel. Each question about other people brings back a lifetime of buried dark emotion.

My father loved me the best way he knew how. We were just very different people and from very different times. His death did not destroy me, but I remember when he died, I systematically went through all the waves of emotions that accompany grief: fear, guilt, loss.

My mother was older than the other kids' moms. It's not a big deal now, but back then people thought she was my granny. My mom was in her midthirties when I was born. I was an "oops" during an affair, and this dark secret was kept from me until after my father's death. Maybe I sensed something earlier, or maybe it was the feeling of not being wanted, but when he died, it hurt but I wasn't devastated.

I was the fourth of five: three boys and two girls. I was expected to act as a grown-up and be far more responsible than is expected of a very young child. I couldn't be a kid. But I had no choice, as I was often left alone. On any given day, I would wake up and my mom would be gone on a last-minute golf trip. I would wait, sometimes for days, until she returned. When she did, I would scold her for being irresponsible and leaving without telling me.

Under these circumstances, I learned to act older than I was and didn't like being treated like a child. This mindset, of course, put stress on all my relationships. My older brothers only visited when they needed something and always treated me like I was inferior and incapable, something that became infuriating because I had learned at home to act as an adult.

There was a point in my childhood when I decided I would cry no more tears for my family. I decided I wouldn't let them hurt me anymore. I was strong enough. I did not need them. It was only many years later, when I was twenty-five, that I cried again. Crying felt foreign, and the emotion that accompanied it was difficult to embrace. I had learned to bury everything. I had to relearn the physical and emotional ability to cry. It doesn't take long for your body to learn new habits, and when you train your body to bury emotion for fifteen years, the journey to re-learning this natural emotional release can be far harder than the event that requires you to cry. I controlled my emotions and held everything in for so long that releasing it was very difficult. I had learned complete control, and to relinquish it felt entirely risky and unsafe.

* * *

My sister started her family when I was five years old. My mom loved and spoiled my nieces, and it seemed like she spent more time and effort on them than me, leaving me to feel even more inadequate. I grew up feeling unfairness in a very deep and profound way that would affect me for the rest of my life. It struck me deeply when I had my own child, to whom she was an amazing granny. Once again, I was reminded of how dismissively she treated me. Now as a mother myself, I struggle to understand how someone can just leave their child at home alone.

Have you ever wondered why certain events follow you in your adult life? Have you downplayed the importance or significance of these events? I sure have! In fact, not only did I downplay the significance but I also absolutely repelled the idea that childhood experiences could have such an impact on or even control over my adult life. I felt I was better than that, stronger than that, smarter than that. Boy, oh boy, was I deceiving myself. That was my ego talking.

Now that I've gone down the rabbit hole of my own healing journey, I know that to be a big fat lie. I now know any unresolved emotions will remain until they are healed, even if that takes a lifetime. Even if my mind has forgotten, my body hasn't. My body

THE GREAT CANADIAN WOMAN

has its own way of storing memories. Yours does too, and grief is one such memory it will store until you're ready to embrace it and learn the lessons it has to teach.

I knew I needed to do something to heal myself. I also knew I wouldn't find the answers at a doctor's office, at a pharmacy, or in a bottle. I learned to practice Reiki and meditation. I began to spend more and more time in meditation and reflection. I spent a lot of time in guided meditations and with Reiki practitioners, then Shamans. I paid attention to the signs the Universe was offering. When my choices resulted in life flowing easily without resistance, I knew I was on the right path. I stopped trying to control every outcome.

As I sat with my own thoughts, I learned how much of our lives are actually created by our thoughts. That life consists of little lies that we tell ourselves. We make them up as children, and we continue doing it as adults. You know the lies: "I'm fine" and "I'm not good enough" and "I'm not worthy" and "I'm not lovable." You think or hear these lies and they eventually become your truth without you even realizing it.

I remember hiding under the stairs in my house for an entire day. I wanted somebody to miss me, I wanted somebody to find me, I wanted attention from my mom. I was there all day and no one noticed my absence. I felt so alone. I felt as if all my fears had been validated.

My sister was everything my mother wasn't. She was eighteen

when I was born. She was my best friend and mother figure. I spent every holiday and summer with her during my childhood. She was my everything, and I hers. She was the only person in life who made me feel special, important, and loved. She acknowledged all my wins and accomplishments. She saw me, she celebrated me, she supported me. My grief was much different with her death than my father's. My world collapsed. Everything about who I was died with her—what I wanted, the life I had planned, and what I thought was important in the future.

Breathing air was something I had to force myself to do, as I felt that I could just stop breathing and then die. After she passed, I sobbed inconsolably on the bathroom floor every night for three months until I just lay there like an incoherent mess. Unlike my father's passing, this one hurt; it felt unbearable.

Grief is a kind of unorganized chaos, a roller coaster that you can't get off. The ups and downs of grief are unpredictable; they are ever changing and uncontrollable. No matter how much you hear about grief, the experience cannot be truly understood until you feel it. I spent my days blankly staring at walls and the nights sobbing. I felt so alone. I wasn't ready to learn the lessons that grief had for me; it would take more time.

I tried therapy. It was a disastrous experience for me. I sat in front of the therapist, whom I was paying, as she spoke about herself and her problems. At the end of the session, she had the nerve to ask, "So, what can I help you with today?" She then giggled a little with the realization of what had just happened. For me, this was validation that no one could help me, that I was alone.

I went to Chapters to try and find books on grieving. At that time, there were few to none available. I left empty-handed on several occasions. I thought I was going crazy, and I was paralyzed in fear that this was my new life. I was afraid that I was doing it wrong, and I didn't know how to help myself. It was at that moment that I decided to write about my experience as much for my own healing as with the hope that it might help somebody else. Writing this story took me years. But one day something changed. I'm not sure what, but something was different. I don't know how I did it, and I don't know when it happened, I just know that one day I felt more like myself. I learned that I had to be gentle with myself, which was difficult for me. I learned it was important to celebrate small wins. All wins are big wins!

After a year I began to feel some control over my emotions, but I was still struggling. It would take more time, and I learned that these moments of residual sadness can happen anytime, anywhere. Over time they become less and less frequent, but they never truly stop. Grief has its own timeline and its own rules. As the days passed, I chose to focus on the parts of my life that I could control. And controlling my life became my focus.

* * *

In the year that followed my sister's death, I got married, got pregnant, and built a house in the suburbs. Strangely, these were all things I said I would never do. These were choices I made in depths of grief. Professionally, I was being fast-tracked to New York. A life of travelling and eating in trendy restaurants was ahead of me. I was on my way to a very successful career, and yet it felt empty and pointless. My successful career was supposed to give me an early retirement so I could live near my sister. We had made plans. We planned to be neighbours, spend our days in our gardens, play cards, and ride our bikes to Starbucks.

Over the next twelve years, my failing marriage and the stress of losing my sister took a physical toll on my body. It started to tell me with very clear signs that I needed to make changes in my life. I spent two years working with doctors looking for medical reasons as to why my body was shutting down. Food was making me sick, I had horrible oozing rashes on my neck, and severe eczema on my hands. Additionally, I would occasionally lose the feeling in my hands. The invisible symptoms were constant as well: nausea, headache, exhaustion, brain fog, and back pain.

I remember my doctor asking me repeatedly if I was stressed. For two years, my response was the same. "I'm not stressed. How can I be stressed?" In my mind there were so many people worse off than I was. How dare I be stressed?! But my body disagreed and let me know clearly. And at forty years old, I had a heart attack.

Thankfully, it was a minor heart attack and there was no

permanent damage, but it was a wake-up call. There were enough abnormalities with my test results to show that something was wrong. My liver enzymes were always out of whack, I had developed severe gallstones, and my digestion was inhibited. So, I made the choice to look inside myself, to start listening to my body, and to stop pushing through the pain.

The more I looked internally, the more I realized that I did not feel loved, valued, understood, or appreciated in my marriage. It was a familiar feeling, as I had felt this my whole life. I was holding back from speaking my truth to accommodate the people around me. There was no joy or happiness in my home or my life. I was simply existing.

After trying unsuccessfully to salvage my marriage, I realized the thought of divorce carried shame, guilt, and sadness, and the shame of failure was the only thing keeping me in it. It was important for me to process all these feelings while in the marriage so that I knew that I did everything possible to save it.

I cried every night. We slept apart, and there was no hugging, kissing, or sex. I had never felt so lonely in all my life, or perhaps I forgot how lonely I had always been. There is a deep and specific heartache to being lonely in a marriage. That heartache vibrated so deeply in my body that I was exhausted and drained all the time.

Anger was my coping mechanism. When you are closed off and angry all the time, you are numb—numb to hurt but also numb to joy and happiness, and the moment I realized that reality was the true beginning to my healing. I had made it through the fog. I was beginning to see the truth. I had my first aha moment. I FINALLY understood why I felt so much anger, and I wasn't angry anymore.

The second aha moment came after my divorce. It came in a moment when all the life stress was gone. For the first time, my life was calm and predictable, but that was new and unfamiliar to me and it made me uncomfortable. It felt like something was missing. I was no longer experiencing those familiar feelings: disappointment, unworthiness, unlovable, and unseen.

I have learned a lot about myself through this journey. I hope some of it will resonate with you. The most important thing to know is that when you live your life simply just existing, it has a cost. The price is happiness. Over time, this choice has physical consequences to your health. If you remember anything about my message, this point is key: "You are only confined by the walls you build around yourself."

Another thing I learned about is the power of grief. If you ignore it, it will consume you. If you can find a way to embrace it with care and compassion, you just may open your heart to yourself and learn how to become free of the prison that grief can become.

These are my experiences. They are no better or worse than yours. Just different. As children, we observe and absorb the world around us in ways we carry for the rest of our lives. We create stories about these experiences, and these stories inform the adults we become.

What I have learned from grief is that memories are more than just thoughts in your mind; they live in your body. These memories can become painful unless you are open to reframing them and learning to forgive. If you can forgive yourself and others for hurt or trauma, then that space inside your heart where the hurt is stored opens up and frees you to experience love and joy.

Nicole Clark

Nicole Clark's journey of death and rebirth is a powerful story that she hopes will inspire others to break through the walls of their own heart so they, too, can find their truth, peace, and joy in life.

For more than twenty years, Nicole has checked all the materialistic boxes in her life: marriage, baby, wealth, and status, yet the cost of this perfection was loneliness and dis-ease.

As a career-driven woman, wife, and mother in this modern society, Nicole considered her emotions to be a sign of weakness. This disassociation numbs us so we can cope instead of speaking our truth.

Simply existing is the creator of dis-ease, and it's time for us to write a new narrative about what is possible when we become resilient and tell our own truth.

Nicole is an advocate of mindful living and hopes to inspire more women to view all experiences as lessons and opportunities for transformation and personal growth.

The bigger the storm, the brighter the rainbow.

In order to write about my life, I had to first experience it. With that in mind, I would like to thank every individual along my journey; each interaction we have has allowed me a lesson and a learning. You have taught me the importance of personal boundaries and have shown me both the person I inspire to be and the kind of person I never want to become. I am so grateful to be awake and mindful on this journey that the best version of myself is attainable. Life is truly about the journey and not the destination. Appreciate every experience and lesson available to you.

To my son, Clark—Your gentle spirit, relentless kindness, and big love means the world to me. Thank you for being the amazing human that you are. I am honoured to be your mom.

To Peter @Thecolourofwater—Thank you for your support in helping me articulate my voice.

Thank you to all the Light Warriors who continue to bravely step forward in service to heal and help others and Mother Earth. May Love find you and Bless you with Grace and Abundance.

To all who wonder if they, too, can change their lives—you can! It takes a conscious decision to listen to yourself and your body without judgment, to love yourself unconditionally, to release control of outcome and expectation, and to embrace your own healing journey.

With Gratitude and Love,

Nicole xo

She Is

Fierce

CHAPTER 10

MAMA, I FINALLY KNOW

Tania Driusso-Belcastro

The cell buzzes, email chimes, the kids are talking, and everyone is wanting something from me at once. "MOM! ARE YOU LISTENING TO ME? PUT YOUR PHONE DOWN FOR A MINUTE. Mom, the world can wait." And for a minute, my son catches my attention. I look up in a blank stare, exhausted and blinking.

Buzz Buzz.

"Okay, I need to answer this now. It's a friend texting. I heard you, I promise. I'll get to that after."

"Help, T, I've been diagnosed. What do I do?" I close my eyes and take a few deep breaths before answering the text.

"It's going to be okay. We are going to get through this together. I am going to help you." A tear runs down my face. My diagnosis plays back like a movie, and my mother's funeral briefly enters my mind. *Shake it off, Tania!* I think to myself.

"Kids, I need to go lie down a bit and rest my eyes." I feel sweat dripping from my armpits, and my heart starts beating faster as I walk toward my room. The dogs lie next to me and give me comfort with silent stares. One puts a paw on my leg. My bedroom, my sanctuary, my place of retreat, the one place I go to curl up in the fetal position and put my headphones in with music on—it is how I always get through pain, a bleed, my kids' visits to the hospital, my mom's cancer. For a few minutes, the world can wait. My favourite song always cheers me up or lifts my spirits like nothing else can. Music brought me back to life and makes my body sway. I lift my hand high to the sky as the music takes over my body, and I start to sing the lyrics with Illangelo and The Weeknd. The door suddenly swings open and startles me as the breeze comes through the balcony and the smell of spring is in the air. I stop, inhale deeply, smile, and take it all in.

Is there a certain smell that can trigger emotions or feelings for you? For me, the smell of blood is a trigger. The smell when you open a package of raw meat. The pungent odour and the look of red meat on a steak bone or dripping on a plate makes me cringe. I started to bleed when I was nine years old. I remained undiagnosed and was passed around from specialist to specialist. I experienced constant procedures and surgeries. Being touched and poked by strange doctors who had no answers, only to be told that I must have a hysterectomy as soon as I could, was devastating. What sixteen-year-old is able to understand hearing this news? I was at the Mayo Clinic in Rochester, Minnesota. Yep, that's where I had travelled to get no answers. Later, I built trust in one gynecologist who not only showed me compassion but also taught me that there is kindness in medical care. My suffering with bleeding and cramping and debilitating pain as a result of endometriosis finally ended when I was twenty-eight, after I had my children and had a hysterectomy. The days of being severely anemic would finally be over, as would my constant worry. Or so I thought! Little did I know my world would change very soon with my children.

A hematologist was brought in the day after my son visited the emergency room with a bleeding nose and rectum to investigate and determine where he could have inherited this disorder. The events of October 28, 2005, echo in my mind because of how he, my youngest, and I are now labelled. The story told to me played on repeat. Like a cinematic scene, I can start and stop it in my brain. "Tania, we have diagnosed you all with a blood disorder; however, you are in an unnamed category. I know this is confusing. You will have medication we can inject you with now or blood products to help control your bleeding. You will have a medical disciplinary team here to assist you, and you will meet with them yearly." What?! I have never felt so alone, and I was angry that my mother was not there to help me through this diagnosis. And when they said not to go home and google stuff—yeah, right! I became the google queen. I don't remember how I drove home that day. I had visions of my mom, nose deep in encyclopedias when we came back from appointments. And now, the guilt I felt from passing this disorder on to my children was overwhelming. I looked in the mirror, cried, and asked God for forgiveness. How did I not know? Why did I not try harder to look for answers after my mom died? I hated myself. I literally collapsed in my husband's arms.

So, I did what I do best and armed myself with knowledge and resources for myself and my kids. It was a new world for us. Nothing was more powerful than learning the word no, and how and when to use it. Through advocating for my kids from city to city, medical teams started helping me realize how powerful and amazing my parenting and coping techniques were with my kids and myself. At times, I sat in silence, upset when one of my sons was bleeding, but silence is powerful. I wiped away tears and just held their hands. I also learned to show my "Factor First" card given to me by my hematology team with all my information written on it to help triage at the hospital, and I never looked back at the waiting room if I was taken in to be seen right away, as I could hear others talking. A wise woman once taught me that *listen* and *silent* have the same letters and there is a time for each. As resentful and angry as I was over the suffering my kids and I had, I knew we could learn and grow from it, just like anything else that would come our way.

As we navigated through the kids' appointments, I was forced to face my own health issues once again. I had a gut-wrenching feeling that I had cancer, but I knew I would be okay. I was hiding my fear because I was trying to shield my family from a world I witnessed when my mother died. A tumour had been slowly growing in my thyroid, taking my voice away more each day. Swallowing became difficult, I gained more and more weight, and I was so exhausted that I felt as if I could sleep forever. I was terrified. I took naps on my breaks to rest my voice. I ate honey to lubricate my voice on calls. I knew I would sacrifice my life for my children, but I wanted to be alive for them forever! I wanted to spend every hour of every day keeping them safe, being here, and giving them confidence. That desire lit a fire in this forty-year-old woman, and I knew then that I could handle anything! Being a mother made me stronger and braver than I could ever imagine. So, I set up the appointments and planned for surgery.

The surgeon decided to only remove half of my thyroid, as the biopsy had been inconclusive. Other than my voice becoming hoarse and some swelling from a hematoma, I tolerated the procedure well. Time feels like it goes by forever when you are awaiting results, especially when you cannot talk much, but I rested and waited for the dreadful sound of "the call" that every cancer patient gets. Then, my phone rang.

"Tania, the doctor would like to see you. Please come in for follow-up results." My heart started racing, and sweat dripped down my forehead. I knew right away that it was not good news. It was only two weeks post-op. Anger took over me right away. I felt like I had been hit by a truck and the only word that escaped my mouth was "shit." "I'm sorry. Yes, coming." I could not talk much, as my voice was not fully back yet. When I met with the doctor, he drew a picture for me and explained that I had a rare form in the 3 percent category called Hurthle Cell Carcinoma and explained what my options were. The good news was that it was encapsulated (it had not escaped outside the bubble), but it did have a tiny hole in pathology. To preserve my squeaky, strained voice, I wrote on a piece of paper: "Take the rest out!"

The doctor said something about the dangers of the surgery, one wrong move and I'd be dead, blah, blah, blah. "Yep, where do I sign?"

* * *

"Tania, Tania, wake up. What's your pain level?" I remember hearing monitors beeping and my name being called, but I just could not come to. Beep. Beep.

"Her oxygen is dropping."

My eyes opened and closed. My chest was heavy, and it felt so hard to wake up. I heard my name and fought to do what they were asking. "Hi," I squeaked.

I was finally stable enough to go to my room, but they were pumping oxygen into me as I was transported. *This is new*, I thought. My husband was in the hallway, and the look on his face was terrifying. It hit me then. This was not normal. Tears leaked out of my eyes. I could barely get any words out as they switched out my humidity mask for oxygen. I was so angry, and I took a picture to remember that moment, as I wouldn't allow any visitors to see me. *So, this is the dangerous part*, I thought. Why can't I talk? Why do I need to ice my neck? I felt so ugly and cold. How did my body fail me?

The first twenty-four hours post-op were just weird, but I got through them! I fought to get some sleep and was just cranky and annoyed. My calcium levels needed to be tested frequently, so the nurses were constantly in and out of my room. Just as I would fall asleep, I would be woken again. But I got some freedom the next day, so I went for a walk, but I had to stop in the bathroom, as I had an overwhelming feeling of suffocating. I threw myself over the sink, while opening the door and ringing the bell for help. Blood. I started coughing up blood. I looked down and saw that my neck drain was clogged. *Shit*. Adrenaline kicked in.

"Keep calm, Tania. BREATHE! DON'T BE SCARED. It's okay, Tania. Come with us. Come back to your room and lie down."

"What is happening? Why can't I swallow water through a straw? Why do you need to crush and thicken everything? Why am I choking?" I was mad and asking questions a mile a minute, but only squeaks were coming out.

"Just rest, Tania, it's okay. We will call the doctor and get him to talk to you." Nurses have a way of just calming you down.

I soon found out that during surgery, my jugular vein had been nicked and sutured, there was bleeding, and my larynx nerve was damaged, causing my voice to go. I folded my hands in prayer and curled into the fetal position with my music on. "God, if you are listening, I need help. I know I should be grateful, but please don't let me bleed anymore and not in front of my kids. Amen."

Rest is the best thing to calm you, but over the next days, I walked the halls, looked out the hospital windows, and thought better days would be ahead if I just followed what my body needed. Once my drain was clear and showed no blood, I was able to leave the hospital to go home and heal. On the drive, I took in the scenery and listened to the sounds of nature. It was like my senses awakened.

Once at home, who had time to think about cancer? I had a hematoma, an ugly zipper of a scar that needed to heal across my neck, and I had to face my family with a squeal of a voice. I banged on pots to get my family's attention, and I hated being in loud spaces because I could not be heard. I couldn't answer the phone for the longest time. Nobody understood what I was going through. How could they? Was this my destiny? I texted as much as I could. I blasted music and felt free when nobody was home. I went to voice lessons. Remember how I said a smell could trigger you? Well, so can a song, and "Fight Song" by Rachel Platten became my go-to song. I hummed and mouthed the lyrics until one day, after nine long months, my voice emerged. I could deal with the medication and the cancer and my new world when I had a voice. I was excited that I could get back to working. Something happens when you start healing. "I think I want to be happy now." Your senses awaken, and your warrior abilities come to life. I have purpose and a calling. It was a second wind. Just me, myself, and I. My fighting gloves came on, and I was ready to deal with everything I had been holding back on.

It was in these moments that I'd catch myself journaling and writing little notes to myself. They are like love notes to myself. This note is for the tiny butterfly gland I never knew I had:

Dear Thyroid, Thank you for trying so hard to survive. I'm sorry cancer overtook you. I'm sorry I never knew what you were meant for. I'm sorry I took diet pills and never thought I was thin enough. I never knew you regulated my weight, my body temperature, my heart rate, and my blood pressure. I just said to get you the hell out, but I never asked, What if you were gone? Now, I need this tiny pill to replace you and save my life every day. I am monitored, as my levels can change. I feel like I'm fighting for my life. Why is my weight all over the place? God, I am so tired. Nobody said I was going to feel like I was hit by a truck on some days! Is this normal? I really don't want anyone to think I am depressed. My body feels like it is falling apart, like a car with no engine. I miss you, Thyroid. I'm sorry I failed you. But thank you for making me a fighter.

∗ ∗ ∗

I sat one day and looked at a tree and thought, *How wonderful you are. You are strong and have roots planted in the ground. You shed your leaves every year. You are not scared when the wind and storms come around to knock you down. You grow branches and a strong bark. How wonderful it is that the birds and bees come to visit, and you continue to grow stronger when someone cuts off your branches. You are not afraid. You don't need much water. YOU can survive in any storm! I want to be a tree!* I envisioned so much. I am your bark, you are my branches, and it's okay if leaves fall, as you will have new leaves, and some will flower! My mentality started to shift and grow. Plant your roots and grow a foundation and amazing things will happen. My engine restarted. I don't need an organ, I need a mindset. I can bring the birds to my tree of life. If I just get out of bed today, it's enough! I'm not a superhuman, but I survived.

I found so many people online who I connected with by just being myself. We could ask each other questions and knew what others were feeling without having to pour out our hearts. Social media is a great tool for finding groups that offer support tailored to what you need. It was a place to be understood without being misunderstood. My confidence started coming back again. We helped each other with questions to ask our doctors. I could ask my new friends about my thyroid medication and even my diet, which helped in other areas of my life. I discovered ACE—the Assisted Cancer Exercise program. It is a wonderful group. I worked out at the University of Calgary and could be myself with other survivors in a non-judgmental class. I was able to build strength and stability, and I learned so much about myself as I grew. Little did I know that these amazing women would give me so much courage and determination to face so much of every challenge head on. With them, I found the courage I needed to move forward on days when I could not put one foot in front of the other. I'm too hard on myself, and I don't like to ask for help. Here, it was easier, as I was in a different setting. I could close my eyes when I went home at night and tell myself not to worry. "You are not going to hit rock bottom." I'd think of my kids and my mother and all she went through with her battle. She was made of strength and generosity. Her love poured down on me, and she pulled me through. I celebrated my victory by getting a tattoo incorporating my mother's name, her cancer ribbon, mine, the rosary for my faith, my kids' initials, and my husband's name. It reminds me that I am never alone. Everyone thought I was so strong during my recovery, but what they didn't know was that there were days I could barely carry on, then I would glance at my tattoo, the fog would clear, and I would be okay.

When you have walked a path, you are able to help others understand and cope when on a similar journey, and you feel empowered and inspired as you help them navigate it. For example, I spoke at Crosscheck for Cancer, a local charity a friend of mine started. I am finding that sharing my journey is so rewarding.

Buzz buzz.

"T, what are the next steps? I have a biopsy." Deep breath. "Don't worry, you are not alone. I am going to stand by you. The results take about two weeks. I'll be your eyes until yours can see, your voice until you know how to speak, and the confidence you need to own this disease. Start a binder to hold your information."

Every scar will tell a tale—a story of a warrior who won a battle. It's okay to ask for help. I started to feel lighter, like an angel dressed in armour.

"T, you're an amazing source of information. I don't know what I'd do without you." This time the tears that escape my eyes are of joy. I am making a difference in someone's life. My heart beats fast, and I know my second chance at life is being used for greatness.

I don't take life for granted. I am grateful when I wake up. I found the more I shared my journey, the more others started to recognize my gifts and even nominate me for little things. I love using my talent for hair styling as a way to help others cope. I love making gift baskets full of products for recently diagnosed patients. I love lending out reading material or just listening. It's a beautiful feeling to be recognized by others, including Leela Sharon Aheer, Alberta's Minister of Culture, Multiculturalism, and Status of Women, or to receive a surprise sign/gift reading "Hell ya for heroes" from a radio station. Others started following me on social media. It is the most amazing feeling in the world to be known as an influencer. My confidence level rose, and now I wear my scars with pride. I learned to be brave, and all my self-doubt has disappeared. Now that I've found my voice again, I will not let anything or anyone get in my way of helping others find theirs. We all start encouraging each other as women, and that is the beauty of being compassionate toward one another. I love to do research, and when I investigated "compassion," I found out that if patients perceive their doctors as caring and compassionate, they recover faster. So, never be afraid to ask for a second opinion if someone is not a fit for you.

I also love to listen to podcasts. Some are so amazing. They lift my spirits and inspire me. They can change my mood. I've learned to focus and envision the life I want to lead and to feel the emotions I want to experience every day. Some days I quiet my mind through meditation. I sit quietly, play music, let my imagination wander, and think about how I want my life to look. Have you ever done this? It's amazing and relaxing. Never be afraid to see how far you've come and be inspired to go a bit further. I took pictures of myself along my journey, of scars, stitches, sadness, and happiness. They are a reminder of how I became this warrior. It's during our most vulnerable points of time when we start shaping the mentor within us. We realize that being silent is just a time to prepare us for the voice that needs to be reborn. It takes tremendous strength to get through what I went through. I still cry sometimes, and that's okay! But it's in these quiet and vulnerable times that you may also find people whom you really look up to—people who are your "sheroes."

My "sheroes" are my grandmother, who is 101 and a COVID-19 survivor, my mother, who passed away at age forty-five, and me! I encourage you to never forget to take time for yourself. Find a career that works around your lifestyle. I truly cannot thank my leaders and mentors enough for being by my side on the days I came back crying from medical appointments, my kids' and mine. They helped me read emails with fresh eyes and understand how to "drop the attitude" when reading them. I became a better mother and employee because I surrounded myself with such positive, strong, amazing women. I absolutely loved the career that allowed me to work around my medical appointments and travel!

Music helped me heal so much, so I travelled to concerts and learned to live again. I could sing and dance and forget about the life that was so full of pain. I turned memories into happy, fun, wonderful ones! Find what works for you. I found a career in aviation so I could work within my love of travel and music, making it inexpensive to enjoy both. Recently, I switched to health care to serve my community during the pandemic. Find a way to make the days brighter, find new journeys, make better memories. Only you can turn your story into something beautiful. I wrote a blog and recorded a podcast to help make a difference in someone's life. Leave a legacy for your kids—one to be proud of!

Don't ever give up. Be proud of yourself! I never stopped learn-ing and researching, and now I feel confident and courageous.

Mama, I finally know . . . I am an advocate.

Tania Driusso-Belcastro

Tania Driusso-Belcastro was born and raised in Calgary, Alberta. Together with her amazing husband, Domenic, they have raised three beautiful children: Lorenzo, Mariah, and Santino. Tania is a cancer survivor who has endured multiple surgeries, endometriosis, and skin cancer, and she, along with her children, have been diagnosed with a blood disorder. Her story has inspired many women. Tania teaches her kids and others to live a whole life, to advocate for one's health, and to never be too afraid to step outside the box. She is known for her random acts of kindness, for encouraging friends to pay it forward, and for working tirelessly to help those in need. She enriches people's lives, both personally and professionally. She is compassionate, resourceful, and willing to comfort friends who require support. Her love of travel and hairstyling has helped many through the toughest of times. She uses social media to advocate for health and to support local businesses. She loves mentoring others and has hopes of one day owning or working for a non-profit to help people fighting disease. Tania wants to encourage you all to always move forward and to never think you are not making a difference in this world.

To all of you—for supporting me every step of the way! The journey is never over, we just add to it. Thank you for picking up this book and reading every amazing story that we all worked so hard to share with you. I encourage you to pay it forward and share it with a friend, to lend it out, or to tell people how to purchase one to support these wonderful authors.

I'd like to thank my husband, Domenic, who has been by my side for thirty-one years and who supports every decision I make. My mother-in-law, Carmena (and Papa Joe in heaven), who stepped in and watched the kids and helped out tremendously. I don't know where I would be today without your love and support. My three kids, Lorenzo, Mariah, and Santino, you amaze me every day. All you have is each other, and you come first always and forever in this world. My father, Frank, and brother, Terry, who believed in me and took a leap of faith to support my journey here in this book. Nonnina Antonia, you are my hero. Thank you for everything in this world you have shown and given me. There are not enough thank yous. Thank you to the Hematology Clinic at the Children's and Foothills Hospital and at Sick Kids for the love, support, and guidance for all of us! Mom, wherever you are in heaven, know this chapter is dedicated to you. I love you. I miss you. I did it for us. Until we meet again . . . Tania

She Is

—— Inspiring

CHAPTER 11

BACK TO LIFE

Gay McFeely

I didn't realize it at the time, but my life was about to change. I am an alcoholic, and I had been out in British Columbia at our condo, drinking myself into oblivion as I always did when I relapsed. I knew that my husband, Gregg, was on a plane at that very moment, flying out to stay at our condo while I would be returning to Calgary. I was scrambling around, trying to get rid of all the evidence. Sadly, I left a case of empty beer cans in a closet, which Gregg ended up discovering.

When Gregg arrived, we had dinner together, and then I left in my rental car to drive to the closest liquor store on the way to the airport. I drank a six-pack in the car on the way, another two at the airport restaurant, and two more on the plane.

The drinking didn't stop there. As soon as the plane landed in

Calgary, I went straight to the airport liquor store and continued to drink on the drive home. As I turned the corner to my house, I was surprised by a police car parked out front and a helicopter hovering overhead. When I pulled into the driveway, I thought that maybe my house had been broken into and they were there to help. But then one of the officers yelled at me to give him my keys.

Out came the roadside Breathalyzer. FAIL. I begged them not to cuff me, but they did anyway, and I was pulled into the cruiser. I was told that an off-duty officer had seen me driving erratically and had called in my licence plate. I knew I was in big trouble.

What followed is in fragments. Fingerprinting and mugshots. An unanswered phone call to my lawyer. A ride home from one of the officers. The discovery that my car was gone, towed to the impound lot. I passed out and woke a few hours later in a state of panic. How would I explain this to my family? How could I escape my thoughts without drowning them out with alcohol? How could I have done this to them again? The shame, guilt, and fear I felt were consuming me, and I felt like I had a rattlesnake wrapped around my neck, strangling me.

I contacted a lawyer who questioned me about what had happened, taking note of a bruise on my arm. I told him one of the officers had grabbed me to put me into the police car. "BINGO. I can get you off, but we will have to go to court. It'll cost you eighteen thousand dollars." A victim of police brutality. Really? I looked incredulously at him and said that I was guilty as charged and had NO intention of fighting the charges.

I knew I needed to come clean to my family, and I was terrified. My eldest son, William, offered to take me to an AA meeting. My younger two children were shocked and disappointed. Gregg had the worst response. As soon as he arrived back in Calgary, he packed a suitcase and told me I was on my own. For a month I ate very little. I was depressed and completely numb, and I felt hopeless and ashamed. I wanted to drink but knew that drinking alcohol was no longer an option. When no one was around, I cried and cried and obsessed about what was to come. Court, conviction, and a five-year criminal record. Never could I have imagined that my drinking would get so out of control.

Gregg eventually returned, but it took time for him to forgive me. He refused to attend court, which I understood. It was my mess, and it was mine to clean up.

Attending court added another level of humiliation. I spoke directly to the judge and expressed my shame for putting others at risk and promised I would take whatever actions necessary to keep myself sober. He thanked me for my honesty. I said goodbye to my sleazy lawyer and told him I was disgusted at his attempt to get me to plead not guilty.

Going through this experience taught me some hard lessons. It took fifty-five years of drinking to finally accept that alcohol could not be a part of my life.

My drinking started when I was around three years old. Hard

to believe, isn't it? My parents would take me out to dinner with them, and I would sip on my mum's favourite drink, a grasshopper, and my dessert was always a creme de menthe parfait, which had around three ounces of liquor in it!

I grew up in a family of alcoholics. There was much chaos in our house. When my dad was sober, he was the kindest and funniest man in the world. When he drank excessively, he became a monster. And when he drank with my mother, he was even worse. The fighting, screaming, and emotional abuse my mum endured was beyond awful. My dad would disappear for weeks at a time. He would sober up for a while after he returned, but the nightmare would always begin again.

On and on this chaotic cycle went until finally, when I was twelve years old, my mum bravely mustered the courage to confront my dad about his alcoholism and kicked him out of the house. Dad went to AA for a time, and my parents even tried to reconcile, but after he continued to relapse, it became clear that they weren't going to get back together. I would live with Mum, and Dad would financially support us. To say I was relieved by the split is an understatement! I was still able to see my dad regularly, but I no longer had to suffer with the turmoil of his alcoholism.

Sadly, their split didn't alleviate my own issues with alcohol. When I was thirteen, I became part of a new peer group, and stealing money and alcohol from our parents was easy and went unnoticed. It was also the first time I became blackout drunk. I was sleeping over at a friend's house and drank an entire mickey of gin. I remember waking up on the floor of her bathroom, humiliated and covered in vomit. I was so relieved that my mother didn't catch on to what had happened. The following weekend I got almost as drunk and passed out on a lawn just a few blocks away from home. The police were called, and I was taken home to my mother, who was so furious that she didn't speak to me for days.

By the time I hit high school, my drinking and drug use had escalated even further. I would try almost any drug or drink that was handed to me, including LSD, Mescaline, and the strongest hashish and marijuana that I could find. I skipped school often, and when I did go, I was usually drunk or stoned.

High school was also where I met the man who would later become my husband. He was two years older, a competitive swimmer, intelligent, quiet, and good looking. He was also a great drinking buddy. Because we were both so introverted, we found it difficult to communicate unless we were drinking. Our dates consisted of driving out in the country and getting romantically drunk together. This behaviour continued through high school, university, and ultimately into our marriage, as we developed a daily pattern of drinking every night after we got home from work.

My drinking stopped as soon as I found out I was pregnant with my first child. Gregg continued. The moment I gave birth and stopped breastfeeding, my drinking would start again. This pattern continued with our second and then third child. Gregg's drinking eventually escalated, and after a three-day binge, he woke up one Sunday morning and said he was going to his first AA meeting. I was shocked and dismayed. I was still breastfeeding my daughter and was waiting in anticipation until I could start drinking again. On November 6, 1992, I went to a couple's meeting with him and acknowledged my own alcoholism. I managed to quit, but the cravings for alcohol never went away. I just refused to succumb to them.

* * *

Just over five years into my sobriety, my mum called and said something was wrong with her vision. The ophthalmologist looked at her eyes and immediately sent her to the hospital. She seemed stunned. She was told that she had a wet form of macular degeneration, it was untreatable, she could no longer drive, and she would likely require in-home support to assist with her day-to-day living! For a woman who had always been extremely independent and was an avid reader, artist, writer, piano player, TV watcher, and wonderful grandmother, this diagnosis was devastating. Reassuring her, I told her that I would always be there to help, but this promise did little to comfort her. In just one month she went from having 20/20 vision to being legally blind.

She continued to have Sunday dinners at her house but drank herself into oblivion at every one. One Sunday she got drunk and staggered upstairs to her bedroom in the middle of the meal. We awkwardly continued eating. Then we all heard a loud crash. I dashed up to find her on the floor, unable to get up. We had switched positions; I was now the one furious at someone else's drinking. I helped her into bed and said we would talk the next day.

"We won't be coming for Easter," I announced to Mum. "I'm taking Marie skiing, and Gregg is going out to the coast with the boys." I also told her that unless she got sober, Gregg didn't want to bring the kids around her. This threat was another blow to her depression, as she regularly watched our children, coming up with imaginative stories and showing them vintage cartoons. She would try, she said, but drinking was the only thing that was helping her cope with the catastrophic loss of her vision. I told her to reflect on it and then hung up the phone.

We didn't talk for a few days. I drove by her house a few times in the evening and saw the blue glow of her computer screen. Good. She was writing, I thought. That was something that comforted her. But I couldn't shed the feeling that I'd done something horribly wrong in confronting her. As a family, we had never directly acknowledged anyone's problems with addiction, preferring instead to remain silent. I was the only one who had the guts to talk to her about it.

My dad started calling. Had I heard from Mum? No. On Good Friday, he went to her house with my sister to check on her, but the house was locked. Could I check on her?

"Sure, Dad, I'll drive over."

All the lights were turned off. Strange. My mother was standing at the end of the hallway. "Mum, what are you doing?" She didn't respond. I turned on the light switch. I looked up to see the extension cord hanging tightly from the upper staircase. She had hanged herself. I screamed and ran over. I felt her skin, hoping it would be warm. It was stone cold.

I called 911, my dad, my brother, and Gregg. The latter two didn't respond; my dad said he'd be there right away. I got down on my knees and prayed for her to be saved.

∗ ∗ ∗

EMS arrived first. No pulse. She was gone.

Dad, victim assistance, and the coroner arrived. They loaded her body on a stretcher and asked if we wanted to see her before she was taken away. My dad stood up, and I told him not to look. He had a heart condition, and I was sure the sight of her death would kill him too. He said, "I know you're going to feel responsible for this." He didn't say, "But it's not your fault." He had not wanted me to speak to her about her drinking. I knew he felt I was responsible for her suicide. My guilt was indescribable.

I tried calling Gregg again. I desperately needed my family with me and thankfully, he answered. Barely able to get the words out, I told him what happened. He immediately woke the boys and started the long drive home. Marie, just four years old, was asleep in her bed. I was alone.

I had five years of sobriety and all I could think about was drinking—anything to block out the pain. I fought the urge with everything I had and even called the Distress Centre. A young woman on the phone told me, "Don't worry. It's hard now, but it will get better."

I spent the rest of the night staring out the window, sleepless and in shock.

My dad arrived the next morning and started making phone calls. Up to this point, I had no tears, but the floodgate finally opened. With each phone call, I broke down further and further. After they were all done, my dad immediately left. I was once again all alone.

Gregg arrived home and we sat the kids down and told them that "Marmar" had passed away. I clung tightly to my family as we all sobbed. Thoughts of drinking crawled back in, but I knew I had to stifle my overwhelming urge now that Gregg was home.

The funeral was awful. I have never cried so hard in my life. My little girl held my hand and told me everything would be okay. I felt everyone's eyes on me, and despite people's compassionate and comforting words, I still felt intense guilt and grief. Afterward, my family gathered at my aunt and uncle's. I watched the beer and wine come out, and all I wanted to do was drink.

But I had small children and a household to run; I had to try to keep it together. I became horribly depressed, so my doctor started me on the first of many antidepressants and benzodiazepines. I'm convinced that's where my first relapse occurred. Just the action of putting something in my mouth to feel better was all too familiar.

After my mum's death, my dad's health began to rapidly deteriorate. I was relieved when he finally decided to have a quadruple bypass. But to our shock and dismay, there were complications and he passed away. In fact, he died almost a year to the day of my mum. I felt like I had killed them both.

My drinking began again that year. My relapse was unintentional; my decision to continue to drink was not. We took a family trip to Mexico with some friends, and one afternoon I ordered a virgin margarita. I took one sip and realized there was liquor in it, but instead of putting it down, I decided to drink it. I said nothing to Gregg about what had happened. I snuck drinks the rest of the trip, with him none the wiser.

I told Gregg that I was going to start drinking again on a casual basis. He said that if I felt I could keep it under control, he didn't have an issue with it. I did manage to control it for several years, but the obsession that alcoholics experience had set in. Whenever I drank, one was never enough. I started hiding liquor around the house and in my car, and I drank at every opportunity. This behaviour went on for years, until I finally completely lost control.

My son Cameron returned from university in Edmonton and was shocked by what had happened to me. He and Marie spoke and decided to hold a family intervention. In June of 2010, I went off to my first of many treatment centres. My eldest son flew out to Vancouver with me, and his last words to me before I left with one of the counsellors were "You can do this, Mum. I'm so proud of you." Watching him go and waving back at me got the tears flowing. What a mess I had made of my life.

I ended up staying for forty-nine days and felt better than I had in years. We had a house in Victoria at that time, and that's where I went when I was released. Marie was already there, and Gregg arrived the next day. I was riding what alcoholics call a "pink cloud," feeling strong in my sobriety and high on life. What I didn't realize at the time was that the elevated mood was my first hypomanic episode from my undiagnosed bipolar disorder.

The following spring, during a trip to California, I started getting floaters in my right eye. Given what my mother had gone through, I immediately sought help at the local hospital. It was a tear in my retina, which was easily fixed with laser surgery, thank goodness! Except it wasn't, and by the next day it was discovered that my retina had detached, and I had to have emergency surgery. The worst thing about all of it was that a nurse innocently mentioned damage to my macula during one of my appointments, and I convinced myself that I was developing macular degeneration, just like my mum had. I was devastated.

A month later, I started having issues with my other eye. It was a long weekend, and I was told that nothing could be done until after the weekend. I woke up the next day completely blind in that eye! I instantly thought the worst and believed I was losing my entire vision. Thankfully, my retinal specialist performed a successful surgery. There were no words to describe my relief!

After I had recovered in Calgary, I told Gregg I wanted to get back out to the coast. We were getting a new puppy from Washington State and had to travel to Victoria to pick him up. Meanwhile, I had fallen into another depression and the urge to drink was all-consuming. I was two years sober at this point. Even getting the puppy didn't elevate my mood. I returned to Calgary at the end of the summer and relapsed again four months later.

I would binge drink whenever I had the opportunity, but I kept getting caught. The relapse cycle had begun, again. I went back out to the coast and drank myself into oblivion. Still undiagnosed with bipolar II, I would drink to try to sleep and bring the hypomania down or alleviate the depressions I experienced every winter. I was barely eating and would only sober up when I knew family were coming. This routine continued for a year.

My last road trip out to the coast prior to sobering up again was the worst. I was completely manic and out of control, drinking in the car while I was driving and not sleeping at all.

After I arrived in Qualicum, I was planning to go over to our cabin on one of the Gulf Islands where several of my family members already were, but I decided at the last minute to stay, giving Gregg the excuse that it was too rough to go across. I drank off and on the entire day, passing out and starting up again. I then brilliantly decided to get something to eat at a fast-food restaurant in the middle of the night. A fight ensued in the parking lot after a car hit me from behind and caused me to bump the car in front of me. Both drivers yelled at me, and I tried to calm them down. Someone must have called the RCMP, and they arrived just after I had gotten my food. A female officer approached my car to ask me what had happened, then asked if I'd been drinking. I said yes but told her it had been a small amount and earlier in the day.

She asked me to get out of the car to do a roadside test, which, of course, I failed. She took mercy on me and said that because I had told her the truth, she would give me a non-criminal suspension for three months. She had my car impounded, took my licence, then drove me home. There I was, once again, left to weave another set of lies not only to evade the inevitable questions about the whereabouts of my car but also to hide my drinking. Would the lies ever stop?

William came over from the island cabin and immediately asked what happened to my car. I lied and said it was at the car dealership being serviced. He believed me and stayed overnight. We went to an AA meeting together, where he received his one-year medallion. I was so proud of him but also so ashamed that I wasn't able to tell him the truth about my own relapse.

The next day, William went back to the cabin and then the questions started to come. Gregg was suspicious about my car so called the dealership, which had no record of it being serviced. He was enraged and didn't want to speak to me about it. He knew something had happened. William, along with my brother, came back over. When I saw their faces, I knew the gig was up. My brother sat down with me and said that they knew everything. They had driven to the office of the RCMP and were told all the details behind the incident. William was furious and started interrogating me. I was so humiliated. My brother finally put a stop to it and asked if I would be willing to go back to treatment. I said yes and that I had already called them for an intake appointment, which was to happen the next day. Thankfully, William calmed down and said he would take me to the treatment centre. As had happened on previous occasions, Gregg wanted nothing to do with it and stopped speaking to me. I heard nothing from him for weeks. The stint in this centre lasted for thirteen weeks. I missed the birth of my first grandchild, spending time with my sister who was dying of cancer, and the death of one of our beloved dogs. I wanted to leave so badly, but knew if I did, I would never regain the trust of my family. Prior to leaving treatment, I had some cognitive testing done and was finally diagnosed with bipolar II. I was put on lithium to alleviate the symptoms.

My story is one that is shared by many. Writing it down on paper has given me an even better understanding that it is possible to recover from addiction, even when you feel hopeless and consumed with thoughts of drinking. It's often the shame and self-loathing that go hand in hand with alcohol or drug abuse, which then prevents you from asking for help. I'm here to tell you that recovery is possible, but you must be willing and honest. You must *want* it with every ounce of your being. Had I remained sober all those years ago when I first found recovery, I could have saved my loved ones from years of distrust, misery, and worry. I had to hit rock bottom to finally accept and be completely honest with myself that there can be no further alcohol in my life.

My family now trusts me again, I can spend time with my sweet grandchildren, and I have no desire to drink anymore. I was two years sober in April 2021. I realize how blessed I am and how alcohol was destroying everything that was and is important to me. I have gotten my life back, and I never want to lose it again.

Gay McFeely

Gay McFeely is a mother to three grown children and two pups, and a grandmother (aka Grammy) to three adorable grandchildren. She has a wonderful semi-retired husband named Gregg, who she met in high school. Her marriage is solid, as are her relationships with her kids, but she has challenged them over the years with her relationship with alcohol, something that nearly destroyed everything that is important in her life.

Thankfully, after a diagnosis of bipolar II and a great deal of soul searching and assistance and support from treatment centres, counsellors, twelve-step programs, friends, and family, Gay now has a life worth living. She has a sober existence with no desire to engage in her addiction anymore. She is eternally grateful to have been given a second chance.

Sadly, she has lost many friends and family members to addiction. She has watched helplessly while they spiralled out of control and finally gave in to the bottle or other drugs. Gay could have been one of them, and she was definitely headed in that direction. Her story is by no means unique but for the fact that she was finally able to come out the other side.

It is her hope that in sharing her story, she might help others who believe there is no escape from their addictions.

I dedicate this chapter to my wonderful family and friends who never gave up on me through all the bad times.

I love you all.

I would also like to thank Shannon Miller who convinced me that I "could."

She Is

——— Grateful

CHAPTER 12

FROM BURNOUT TO BREAKTHROUGH

Julie Brooks

The calendar on the refrigerator was colour-coded with my work schedule, kids' activities, birthdays, and appointments. It felt like there weren't enough hours in the day. I barely had time to get groceries, prep lunches, make a meal, do laundry, clean the house, do homework, or bathe the kids, let alone take five minutes for me. I would tell myself repeatedly, "You can do this, just get through to the end of the day." I didn't want to complain, and I just kept thinking to myself, *Who would listen to me anyway?* After all, I had chosen this path. Society teaches us to believe that we must suffer some kind of consequence to succeed. Get good grades, study hard, apply to post-secondary, graduate, get a job, get married, have babies, go to work, buy a big house. Do all those things well and you can have everything your heart desires. Isn't that what is considered living the dream? I was a perfectionist, a type A personality, and that "dream" was the story I had told myself and for so long. I made lists in my head and on paper (just in case I forgot something), but this habit ultimately created more chaos in my mind. I just kept trying to check off all the boxes. I believed that I had to be present for everyone and everything. Most of the time, I couldn't concentrate or focus. I was constantly busy, feeling overwhelmed and living in fear, desperately trying to control everything at home, in marriage, with the kids, and even at work. I had created these expectations of myself. I told myself that I had to be productive and push harder. Ultimately, I was just causing more stress.

I was in my early twenties when I decided to get married and then finish my last year of school. After I returned from a short honeymoon (just a weekend away), I was visited by a friend who was home from university. She knew right away. She said, "You're glowing. Are you pregnant?" That evening I had a plus sign appear on the pregnancy test. Nine months later, my honeymoon baby arrived. She has always been so loved; however, at that moment in time, having a baby wasn't the short-term plan. Less than one month after I delivered, we hired my sister to be her nanny. I received permission to work 3:00 p.m. to 11:00 p.m. so I could spend the day with my baby, all while I completed my clinical hours to obtain my nursing diploma. My then-husband worked nights, slept all day, then would wake up, eat, hug the kid, and leave.

I was determined to be the perfect mother and wife. I constantly sought out the added support of my sister and both sets of grandparents. I wanted to make my marriage work, but I felt like a single mother most of the time. I was hired part time at the hospital, and I picked up shifts whenever they were offered. We built a new home and moved to a better neighbourhood. Three years passed, and I continued to struggle with trying to do it all. I often lied to myself by thinking, *It has to get better*. I pleaded with my husband to have another child, and I got pregnant. My second daughter was an irritable baby. She had colic and cried constantly, and I was exhausted. I felt depleted and alone, and it wasn't until several years later that I realized how my emotions had affected her. I stayed busy, going on bike rides, taking the kids to the park, playing outside with neighbours, and driving to visit my parents every chance I could. Between work and the household responsibilities, I was like the Energizer Bunny who just kept going and going. But I was running on empty, and deep down I knew it wasn't sustainable. Family and friends now tell me that they could see the pain and hopelessness in my eyes back then, but I wasn't about to admit those feelings to anyone at the time, not even to myself.

There were many times I recall driving home from work in a complete daze after a shift at the hospital where I had given 110 percent to my patients and their families. I would be dehydrated, my urine dark brown, and in many instances, I wouldn't have even taken a break or had time to eat. It felt like I was driving early in the morning in a dense fog. Have you ever driven from point A all the way to point B and then thought, *How the f**k did I just get here?* I felt drained and completely numb on most days. I was afraid to acknowledge my feelings, so I just ignored them. I pushed them deep down to the very depths of my being. I tried to give what little I had left to my children or to my husband, and many times I wondered, *Am I the only one who feels this way?* Have you ever just said that you're fine when you weren't because you didn't think people would understand?

I distinctly remember a specific moment in time. It was my day off, and I had a list to tackle and was determined to complete it. If I accomplished all the things, then I would give myself permission to rest. I can still see my girls sitting on the couch watching cartoons: "Mommy, are you going to play with us soon?"

"In a minute." But that minute never came. I so desperately wanted to spend quality time with them, but I was emotionally and physically drained. All the struggle, hopelessness, and frustration I felt was almost unbearable, and I had been suppressing these feelings for so long that they began bubbling up like a volcano ready to erupt. My heart was beating out of my chest, I had a lump in my throat, and tears began running down my cheeks. I ran upstairs so my girls wouldn't see me. I judged myself by thinking that in no way was it acceptable for my girls to witness me in a moment of weakness.

That evening after I settled them into bed and knew that they were asleep, I found myself lying in bed feeling defeated. I started a bubble bath, climbed in the boiling hot water, and sobbed uncontrollably and then fell asleep. When I woke up, the water was cold. Shivering, I climbed out, put on my robe, and lay down on the floor. I was so exhausted that I slept there until morning when I asked myself, "What have I done to deserve this?"

I just kept lying to myself, pushing myself, and pretending that everything was perfect. In reality, I was about to fall apart.

My aha moment came when I realized that things were not going to change. Acknowledging that I wasn't happy in my marriage was one of my biggest truths, a turning point in my life, an awakening for me. The Universe was nudging me one step closer to cultivating the strength and courage to face my fears and begin again. The next day I called a friend and told her that I had made a decision. I didn't want to disappoint anyone and was worried what everyone would think or say, but as difficult as it was, I was going to end my marriage. I recall screaming and fighting with my husband when I told him. The girls were playing outside on the swing, and they tell me now, many years later, that they could hear us. But it was the best decision I ever made. I promised myself I would create a new life, a happier life with my girls.

I moved back in with my parents, as it was the only way to save some money to move forward. I am eternally grateful for the love and guidance they provided to me and my girls through some of the most difficult times in my life. I continued to work two part-time positions at the hospital, while my parents assisted with meals, homework, and getting my girls on and off the bus. At that time, I needed a full-time position, so I applied for the job of float nurse, which required me to work on a different floor each day. It was hard work. I woke up early, stressed about where I was going: Medical, Surgery, Emergency. It was difficult working with different personalities every day and to process even simple tasks. I had to build a rapport with staff and patients, and I had to stay focused on giving medications, communicating with families, and answering all the call bells. The amount of stimuli in that environment was a lot to process. I was basically the "sick bitch." My internal voice told me to put on my happy face and focus because no one could ever know what was going on at home.

I was determined to utilize the tools that my workplace and friends suggested. I made regularly scheduled appointments to work through my anxiety, trauma, and grief. The kids went for colour therapy and attended a couple of counselling sessions, but they were discharged quickly as they reassured me that I had an amazing support system and they didn't need to continue. I, however, continued with sessions for many months and years. When I left therapy, I was told to seek guidance as needed and to reach out when things arose.

Recovery is such a monumental task. It's for the brave souls who admit they need help and do the work to get there. It took years of counselling and a journey of deep inner healing to even begin to forgive myself. I survived some of the hardest moments alone while everyone believed I was fine.

I never wanted to admit that I was suffering, but as time went on, I learned that I needed to love myself in order to love another. I had to be brave and take one step at a time. I began to heal. I started to enjoy the little things again. Eventually, I fell in love and remarried. We moved in together and co-parented four kids and supported each other through many years of ups and downs. Life finally felt like it was coming together, until it fell apart again.

It was a Friday, and I had just arrived at work when the supervisor requested to speak with me in an office down the hall from the nurses' station. I opened the door, and two officers were standing in the room. My heart sank, and my stomach tied in knots. My father had been in an accident. "Is he in Emergency? Take me to him."

"We are sorry, ma'am . . . he's dead." I was in complete denial. I screamed and shouted, demanding to drive myself home. I called my husband, tears streaming down my cheeks, barely able to speak. "My dad was in a motorcycle accident, honey. He's dead."

Several days later, I found myself sitting in my backyard alone for the first time. That morning I had taken a long shower, and my husband had made coffee for me. For the first time in a long while, I was enjoying the present moment and savouring the taste of my coffee. I had told my husband the night before that I wanted to sleep in, so he arranged for the girls to be picked up by friends.

They needed some time to process too. Their absence allowed me the space to just take the day to sit and be. I felt the warm sunlight shining down and the soft breeze blowing through my hair. And in the distance, I could hear the birds singing in the trees. There was nowhere to go, nowhere to be. I began to sense a deep calm, and in that moment, I felt my father's presence beside me. It was as if a movie played slowly in my mind as I sat reflecting on the memories: My father watching the kids play in a pile of dirt, teaching them to fly a kite and to skate on the pond in the winter, and taking them on the four-wheeler to the back of the farm to look for deer.

I could see myself talking to him (like I had so many times before). He would be tinkering on a project in his shed, and he would just listen. Talking to him had been a form of therapy for me. He always encouraged me to slow down and reminded me time and time again to enjoy the little things—to pick a moment in time, something that would make me smile that day. I didn't know how important his advice was at the time. It would irritate me and make me angry. But what he shared was truly profound, and it changed who I am as a mother, daughter, sister, niece, co-worker, and friend. It was on that summer day that I finally realized, after so many years of constantly striving for more and achieving most of it, that it was up to me to choose PEACE.

On day four of my bereavement leave, I was about to settle into a chair and begin processing all of my emotions. The phone rang, and my husband was visibly irritated when he opened the patio door. "It's work." *Really, they're calling me right now?* I had just started to feel again after being in absolute disbelief over the last few days. I was overcome with frustration, and I could feel the anger rise up within me.

"Hello, I'm sorry to bother you right now, but are you available for an extra shift tomorrow? We are calling in for overtime."

I was speechless. Then out of the very deepest parts of my being, I began to lose it. I shouted into the phone, "No! No! and No! Absolutely not! I'm not coming in, and I'm certainly not coming back to work tomorrow." I slammed down the phone and began to sob uncontrollably. My husband gently wrapped me in his arms.

"It's okay, honey. It's going to be okay." We sat there together in silence.

The truth is that the trauma of losing my dad had shaken me to the core. I had lost a piece of my heart. A piece of me changed forever. I began to think about my mother and many family members and friends—all of whom had been touched by his presence. We would continue to live without him, as so many others do when a loved one dies, but when you lose someone unexpectedly, it just doesn't make sense. Having the time to be at home and reflect after the funeral was truly a gift, a new way of living my best life. I vowed to myself that I would be more present. I would find joy in the simple things: a bluebird, a dove, a butterfly, a rose.

Moments of crises are times to grow.

Less than a week after the funeral, I was scheduled to return to work; however, I was only beginning to process what had happened. I decided to make an appointment with my family doctor. I had been finding it difficult to concentrate at work, even prior to my dad's death. I knew something wasn't right. I begged the doctor to give me a few weeks to spend time with my daughters and to work on my mental health. When I explained to him that I was experiencing all the signs and symptoms of burnout, he did not appreciate me as a nurse, let alone a woman, self-diagnosing. I urged him to give me a bit of a break, but he snickered and laughed at me and said, "Suck it up, buttercup. You're a nurse and people need you." He refused to write me a note for an extended leave of absence. I reminded him about how there were high expectations of me at work and at home. I was the float nurse, which meant I did not have a core group of women to support me upon my return. I reminded him about the symptoms I had had the previous year: numbness in my face and down my right leg, which caused me to be off from work for about a month. Several investigations had been done: ultrasound, X-rays, and an MRI, and I believed I was in some type of adrenal fatigue or a thyroid storm. The signs were all there again, but the doctor refused to acknowledge them and demanded I head back to work. I am proud to say that I have not returned to him.

This experience fuelled me to find alternatives to get better. I went home and shared my plan with my husband. He supported me 100 percent. I made an appointment to see a naturopath, and after blood work and several visits, my beliefs were confirmed. I was experiencing symptoms of adrenal insufficiency, and further testing verified a rare autoimmune disease. Adrenal insufficiency is a condition in which the adrenal glands do not produce adequate amounts of hormones, primarily low cortisol (the stress hormone) due to chronic stress. Deep down I had felt the dis-ease in my body. It was time for me to take action, and I was open to whatever the naturopath would suggest. Part of me felt a sense of peace having found someone who would listen to and help me seek out the answers I so desperately desired. The old Julie may have just ignored the symptoms and kept pressing onward with the hope that they would just disappear. However, my newfound intuition knew better. Ultimately, I was off work for over a month and without pay because I needed a medical doctor's note with a specific diagnosis, and the naturopath's note had been deemed insufficient. When the month was over, it was with deep apprehension and a need to provide for our family that I decided it was time for me to return to work. But this time, I wasn't going to fall into the same pattern.

Change can be subtle, yet it can make a profound impact. I started dedicating time to focus on my healing, and I began to experience more ease and flow in my days. It had been almost a year since my dad passed, and I was beginning to carve out small windows of time for myself. I regularly booked massages, and I participated in restorative yoga classes after work. The studio was close to home, and there I was able to connect and surround myself with like-minded souls who continue to support me in my business to this day. A simple inhale and exhale while lying in savasana (flat on my back) on a yoga mat is where I took rest. I just rested on a mat and breathed, and it allowed me to feel on a deeper level. I also took simple steps like treating myself to tea and walking around a bookstore where I would intuitively pick a book and read part of a chapter. I began to journal. I'd ask myself what I wanted to do on my day off, what I wanted to eat, whether I wanted a coffee or tea, what colour I wanted to wear, who I would like to visit, where I would spend my time and, most importantly, how I wanted to feel. These small changes in my day-to-day life made an enormous impact on how I felt internally.

I was invited by a dear friend, a mentor and coach, to attend a local event. I instantly felt my heart skip a beat. I could hear this voice shouting in excitement, "Just do it!" So, I called in sick that day. This event is where I started to see that there were other women just like me. I could connect and see a bit of myself in each of their stories. For the first time in a long while, I didn't feel alone. Three leaders from the community came together to bring their individual gifts. It was an amazing day. We spent the morning listening to one of the leaders speak and share her story, and we ate nourishing food and connected. We were asked to bring a journal, and I began to write down my biggest fears as well as some of my deepest desires. I made a conscious decision to make changes. I learned that I could not just continue to survive but that I had a deep desire within me to thrive. That weekend shifted something deep inside of me, and I began the journey to find the deepest parts of myself. I am eternally grateful for the opportunities the Universe granted me and for the beautiful souls who continue to inspire me.

At one time, even taking five to ten minutes for myself was difficult, and someone suggested that I read Gabby Bernstein's book *May Cause Miracles*. Years later, I realized how important it is to take time for yourself. It takes forty days to create a habit. In her most recent book, *Super Attractor*, she states, "The main way we block our desire is by believing we are not worthy."[1] This idea really hit home for me. I am a recovering perfectionist. I have learned that if I just set aside a few moments each day, I can create an opportunity to lean in and dig deeper. I have worked through many emotions and now find time daily to meditate and reflect. Some days begin with five minutes, ten minutes, even up to an hour in sacred space. There is no right or wrong way. I am most uplifted by meditations, journaling, yoga, reading books, and listening to podcasts. I love to create opportunities to give myself and others a reason to connect. I now say yes to what I desire and no to what doesn't feel aligned. I am finally living my life authentically.

It is in stillness that I am able to inhale and exhale, be in the moment, and listen to my intuition—that still, small voice that guides me on my journey. This is my passion. There was a day when it dawned on me while lying in savasana, tears streaming down my face. I had forgotten about all the worry and the stress and anxiety in my life. My tears were tears of gratitude for the growth that has taken place inside my soul. I had been so worried and so consumed about getting everything done, but in that moment I realized I was in my sacred space.

In the years following my father's death, I would be driving, and a song would come on the radio: "Stay Humble and Kind" by Faith Hill and Tim McGraw. Hearing it hits me so deeply that sometimes I still can't control the tears. And it is in those moments when all the memories come flooding back that I truly miss him the most. Grief comes in waves: a divorce or the death of a parent, grandparent, or even a patient. These are the moments that have truly changed the way I choose to live my life daily.

In the end only three things matter: How much you loved, how gently you lived, and how gracefully you let go of things that are not meant for you.

~Gautama Buddha[2]

Julie Brooks

Julie Brooks is an integrative wellness coach from a small town in southern Ontario.

Working as a registered nurse for more than twenty years, her passion for caring about others has grown. She dedicates her time to helping women create more energy in their lives for what truly matters.

Julie has faced many challenges throughout her lifetime: self-doubt, stress, grief, and burnout. She ignored her emotions for years until she made a brave decision to start listening to the internal guidance of the heart. This step was the first of many that allowed her to begin following her intuition on a path to find peace. She has now made it her mission to help guide other women on their healing journeys.

When Julie isn't holding sacred space for others, she loves connecting to nature, and she can be found walking on local trails or meditating in her favourite spot near the lake. She loves vacationing with her husband, especially when the trips involve long walks and scuba diving. Julie finds her serenity deep within the ocean.

Julie is an inspiration and a guiding light for others. She has been a guest speaker at local events, she has appeared on podcasts, and she offers many energy healing modalities. Additionally, she leads online workshops and has hosted weekend retreats. She encourages like-minded women to shift their mindsets and embrace the way they want to feel by moving from a place of surviving to truly thriving.

To all the beautiful souls who have encouraged and supported me on my journey thus far, thank you. You know who you are.

To my husband, Jason. You are my best friend and my rock. You support and encourage me every day to follow my dreams and to share my light with others. To my girls, Emma and Hannah. You are the inspiration for me to feel deep within my soul to inspire you to dream and become the independent women you are. You are the greatest gifts I have ever received.

To my mom. You hold the true meaning of what it is to be the pillar of bravery and strength. To my father who isn't here to read this chapter. I feel your spirit with me, always.

She Is

Strong

CHAPTER 13

CONDITIONS OF THE HEART

Sarah Ozmond

It was the first time I had felt anything in what seemed like a lifetime, whether physical or emotional. I was there, at the firepit in my backyard, and the anger and frustration had built up enough that I started whipping my beer into the fire. Reaching as far behind my back as I could, I continuously threw it toward the flames, creating an arch of liquid over my head. Soon, the back of my shirt was soaking wet. I remember the fluid, almost graceful motion of peeling my shirt from my body and connecting it to the fire while saying, "Sean hated this shirt anyway." Then I went into our house and dug out an old purse I knew he wasn't a fan of, dumped the contents onto our bedroom floor, then walked with intent back out to the yard to sacrifice it as well. I did have friends there with me, but the only voice I remember hearing at that moment was my own. "He hated this too." My friends loved me too much to draw attention to my behaviour or to make me feel crazy, so they just went with it. In fact, they supported me.

The timeline is deviously blurry, but I do know this event occurred within days of the funeral. It was the first time my body had released me from the hold of my adrenaline long enough to feel the effects of the alcohol I had been drinking. I was thankful for that moment, knowing the road ahead would be long and agonizing, and I needed a break from that thought. I had tried for many days to numb myself from the pain of losing the love of my life, mainly by drinking a lot more than I was eating but also by allowing myself to be distracted by all the people surrounding me. It turns out that adrenaline beats alcohol in a good majority of fights, at least in me. At least until that night. So, there I was, shamelessly sitting around the firepit shirtless, breasts bursting out of my dirty lace bra. I didn't care that there were people with me, nor did I think for a moment about what they thought or how it would make them feel. Man, I miss that feeling (or lack thereof, I guess). Even at such a consuming and traumatic time, I remember thinking how freeing it was not to care.

It had been a long, sleepless few days leading up to the surgery. On the day of the surgery, Sean's brother, sister-in-law, my brother, and a couple of close friends were with us at the hospital. The operation took hours longer than expected, and there was a lot of internal bleeding that they had trouble getting under control.

Sean went into the ICU post-surgery, and the surgeon came and told us that he was not out of the woods yet. He then proceeded to remind me that he had warned us of this risk during our pre-op consultations. It was a well-worded "I told you so."

So, we waited. Finally, the nurse came to us and said he was stable and that we could see him. We felt calm, relieved, and hopeful when we saw him looking so peaceful and beautiful. After a short time, we were told to get our rest and to give him his. We could call and check on him at any time, and even visit him if we were staying, but because it was the middle of the night, we should try and get some sleep so we could be there for him later. So, everyone dispersed, and I went to the single bathroom around the corner from the waiting area, fell to my knees on the stained tile floor and, filled with fear and desperation, prayed. I'm not sure who I was praying to . . . God, the Universe, anyone who could hear me . . . but from the core of my being and the depths of my soul, I begged for Sean to live. I don't remember much more, but I won't easily forget that feeling of pleading to keep my love alive—our time together couldn't possibly be over, the thought was unfathomable, and no loving Universe would do that to us.

My brother and I decided to spend the night in the waiting room of the hospital instead of the nearby hotel. There was something in me that couldn't bear to leave Sean alone, something linking me to him that I couldn't deny. The waiting room had multiple couches where a couple of other hopeful people were trying to relax. The hospital staff gave us blankets and pillows, so my brother and I settled in as best we could, and for the first time in days, after seeing Sean and feeling some relief, we finally fell into a remarkably deep sleep.

And then the phone rang.

I'm sure I've never been so startled. I ran to it, barely able to focus and not knowing where I was. "Is this the Williams family? You need to come down here right away."

My brother and I stumbled, feeling our way down to the ICU. From what I remember, we were greeted by a doctor who told us they had been trying to resuscitate Sean for forty-five minutes, as he kept coming back and then they would lose him again. All I heard was that he was trying to live. They wanted us to know they were now stopping the resuscitation attempts . . . phrases including *brain damage* and *difficult decisions* swirled around my head. Someone then proceeded to push us into the room where Sean was, just as they called the time of death. The doctor who had been frantically working on him closed the curtain, as I'm sure we were not supposed to be there. Then numerous people pushed us in different directions until there I was, sitting with his lifeless body, holding his still-warm hand and feeling my brother's grip on my shoulder. Sean was gone. In this horribly surreal moment, he looked exactly like himself. His beautiful lips and skin. Even his hair was in place. The pain was instant and bottomless, from such depth that I didn't even know existed. My entire being gasped in disbelief and heartache. My lifetime's most profound sorrow and most fulfilling joy came from the same person. The only words I could muster were "No, Seany. No, Seany. No".

It's very rare that I allow myself to go back and think deeply about that day in the hospital. In fact, it's when those feelings begin to arise that I tend to use my newfound power of redirecting my thoughts so that I don't fall too far into the dark place that can so easily consume me . . . that place grievers know so well. The place that drains our energy, makes us feel hopeless, and has us question why we bother to go on at all. It's like being in the water but staying close enough to the surface that you can see the weeds but cannot touch them. You remain up where it's safe from what's lurking at the bottom of the cloudy lake. When I think of how hard I work sometimes to keep those memories away and what it does to me when they do seep in, I often think of my brother and how he must be doing something similar so as to avoid reliving that pain. I could not have survived Sean's death without him and will be forever grateful that he was there. At the same time, I will never take for granted the images and damage he, too, will have to carry from being there with me that day—from losing a brother and from watching me go through the most painful moment of my life.

Sean had had a heart condition. He was born with it, and he was told at a young age that he would not live to be a very old man. He had his first open-heart surgery as a toddler, and his next as an adult about five years before we met/reconnected. I don't know if it was Sean's early diagnosis or just him being who he truly was, but he lived life to the fullest like no one I've ever known. He was dynamic, adventurous, so very talented and funny, generous, and someone who everyone just wanted to be near. I've never had more fun with anyone in my life, and I know many people he touched throughout his short journey would say the same. I wish he could know how much he affected so many people's lives because I don't think he had any idea how powerful he was.

So, there we were, living our happy, blissful, carefree life together, two and a half years into our three-year relationship, when we were told he needed to have yet another surgery, an operation that should not have come about for at least ten more years. We were robbed, he was robbed, and even knowing that, never for one moment did any of us think that he wouldn't make it. Sean's previous surgery had been done so poorly that not only did the world-class surgeon doing this one express multiple concerns about performing the operation, he was also unable to fix the mess left years earlier. There's something about knowing that Sean's death was preventable, that if everything had been done correctly the first time, then the outcome could have been different. That thought has always haunted me.

My brother and I arrived home from the hospital in the early morning hours. I don't remember how or when or even who came first, but my yard started to fill up with people. It was abnormal and bizarre to me and yet somehow the most beautiful thing. It was as though without Sean, they didn't know what to do. There had to be sixty or seventy friends and family members there. There were hugs and tears and condolences, and there were drinks and stories; it was almost like an instant wake for all the souls now lost without him. People gathered like we had always done, trying to hold on to one last "Sean moment" before they had to carry on deprived of him. This whole action was a true testament to who he was as a man, friend, and human, and as odd as it all was, in some ways it felt strangely normal. I wandered from one person to another like a bewildered zombie in a pinball machine, saying stupid shit like "I'm so glad you're here." In reality, I had no idea what was happening. Truly though, whether it was for the distraction or just having some sort of a direction, I really think I was glad a lot of them were there.

I can't imagine how difficult and bizarre this time must have been for my parents. They somehow kept everything under control while still allowing it all to happen. Meanwhile, they had lost someone who was like a son to them; in fact, they lost the only man who had been in my life who they truly loved. I took phone calls from people who had learned of Sean's death from a social media post made by one of his family members. Calls from people close to us who deserved to hear the news in a completely different way and wanted to know if it was real. It still angers me to think of it. I should have had the chance to tell them, or at the very least they should have heard it from a human. Instead, Sean's death became about who could be the first to announce it.

That day went on way too long. Finally, I found myself sitting at a table outside with the last people . . . the ones who didn't want to leave, who had even made it a bit of a party. I decisively said to myself, "What the fuck am I doing sitting here like this trying to make all of you feel better. This is ridiculous," and I went to bed. My brother tucked me in, and we had a tearful exchange. I'm sure he and my sister-in-law stayed the night, not that I remember anything, and that was it. I spent my first night without Sean. I'm so glad I don't remember it. Something that did stay with me was when we were at the burial. A close friend's mother said to me, "Oh, honey, you won't remember any of this," and she was right. I don't remember a lot, and even what I do remember is blurry. It has been said that a traumatic loss is similar to a brain injury in the way it affects your memory. Your brain rewires itself to deal with the shock. This comparison makes so much sense to me. When I try to remember timelines or details, names or even basic day-to-day things, I can't recall them. And this memory loss isn't just post-trauma. It's also managed to erase or at least confuse some things from before I even knew Sean, perhaps in part because I fight so much to hold on to our memories and therefore forfeit specifics from a time I care less about.

The next few months were an absolute blur of tears, pain, stomachaches, and fake smiles. I had to force myself to leave my house. I fumbled through birthdays, anniversaries, holidays . . . milestones that would take me down for the next few years. It took two months before I would drive my car due to a newfound anxiety. Everyday things like grocery shopping, running errands, or going out for lunch became stressful, demanding, and brought on panic. Sometimes I'd drive places, feeling quite proud that I got out and ready to take a step back to normalcy. Then I'd find myself sitting in my car in a parking lot, heart racing and breathing rapidly, until I'd just turn the car back on and drive home to safety. I was really afraid of triggers that would debilitate me in public or, worse yet, running into someone who didn't know Sean was gone and having to say the words out loud. I'm happy to say that I did get better and truly just needed time to let my brain adjust to why I was feeling that way; I needed time to realize it was all just part of what I was going through and not something permanent. I also started a bit of a journal. I found that it wasn't when I was at my most desolate that I wrote, as in those moments, I could barely function. I wrote at times when I felt like I had to get something out of me . . . something nagging. I've looked back and read the entries a number of times over the last few years, and as difficult as it is for me to hear my voice in that small, inconsolable tone, it's also a little bit empowering when I realize that I'm still functioning on this planet every day.

There are so many levels to each underhanded, emotional wave that comes and goes. Everything is bigger; every part of life and every stress and loss from now on is compounded to create an even larger swell. It's like when a bird flies overhead and the shadow it casts on the ground is enormous, yet the bird itself is so small. For some of us, it's really difficult to admit we're struggling, as we want to be the helpers among our people. We become these amazing actors on life's stage who can smile through the discomfort, who can still manage the big laughs and to be a part of everything . . . even overcompensate so no one can read between the lines of the script. We refuse to play the victim and have mastered an emotional game of chess. We are always one step ahead until the exhaustion can no longer be ignored. I'm still tired all these years later.

I've spent many moments throughout the last four years wondering about my mental state and whether I'm actually crazy. I found myself talking out loud as if Sean's still here, saying things like "Did you see that?!" when our dog was being extra cute, or literally greeting a cardinal or a breeze, convinced it must be him reminding me he's here with me. I constantly spoke to him, especially when I was out walking the dog. Something about being outside in nature made it feel like that was our time together. I talked to him like it was a one-sided catch-up. I'd fill him in on things and beg for signs that he could hear me, then think he had if suddenly I could see deer in the woods. I talked directly to photographs of him too, sometimes for so long that I could swear his expression changed. I've definitely had some moments, and if you're wondering, the answer is yes, I still do a lot of these things, even now. The truth is, though, I'm not crazy, not at all. I'm grieving and terrified. I am adapting to a new life and a future I'm unsure of, missing the past yet more afraid of going forward. My sense of calm has disappeared; my non-judgmental sounding board no longer exists. I struggle to put into words what it feels like when the person you wake with, sleep with, eat, breathe, laugh, fold laundry, make plans, and choose to spend your life with is just not there anymore, not anywhere.

I've also spent time wondering when I'd get back to the "old" me, the person I was with Sean or even before him. As much as my core values and personality traits remain, I also now know that the person I was before now, untouched by devastation, no longer exists. It would be impossible to go back after this experience, this knowledge. But that's okay too. I need to be who I am now to move forward, to create my own path, and to hopefully be there to help anyone who needs hear that they're not crazy and that their life will carry on. I don't want to be the same person I was, really. She was often more concerned about how other people felt and chose their comfort over her own. I will always be someone who is happiest when those around me are content, but I don't think that's abnormal for anyone. The difference is that now when I look back on my life, I'm angry, livid, in fact, at the choices I made to put others before me at times that I shouldn't have. I think of the times I wasted so I wouldn't make someone else uncomfortable. The positions I allowed myself to be in so as to not embarrass people who clearly did not care about what they were doing to me. The moments when I was at my lowest, saddest, and most devastated and still catered to others while remaining polite and well-mannered to make them feel better as they took advantage of my weakness. I made excuses for them, citing what dreadful things they were going through in their own lives and therefore surrendering and diminishing my own pain, my own self. Now, I refuse to be that person again, and it is all directly due to life-shattering experiences.

Grief will allow you to heal in your own way and rebuild yourself and your life, but it will not let you stop grieving or be the same as you were before. But you shouldn't be the same, and that is okay. I can't imagine that we are meant to survive these life-altering occurrences just to remain exactly the same people we were prior to them. I won't pretend to have the answers, but I will say that I think if we allow ourselves to, we can learn something from all of the bullshit . . . we can take away something we may not have found otherwise. For some, this thing will come swiftly and obviously, and for the rest of us, it will take time. Either way, the one thing I've confidently learned so far in this journey is that it is completely okay and, in fact, necessary to not be the person I was before. It may be the only way for me to discover my true self, my inner power and strength that I didn't even know existed. It may be the only way to find the will to navigate the hardest moments and to still come out the other side.

I have wonderful people in my life. I have loyal, loving friends who stood by me and still do. I have the very best family a human could ask for, something I've known and been grateful for my entire life. I'm also lucky enough to have a very close friend, someone who I trust with my all, a friend who has been through a similar loss and who I can talk to about everything. She makes me feel normal, sane, human. Her honest, no-fluff approach to life is what I need and appreciate the most. Everywhere else I turned for help was like reading a textbook written by someone who had just finished reading another textbook. People would say that grief was a deeply personal experience and that no two were the same, but it was like they didn't believe it and would try to lump us all into one bucket. This approach may be comforting to some, and I'm by no means knocking anyone else's methods at all, it just didn't work for me. It made me think that what I was feeling wasn't right and that I wasn't where I was supposed to be in my journey or process.

My friend and I talk openly about how we feel when other people say things like "I know exactly what you're going through, I'm divorced" or, only months after our loss, "You seem better." When I share how much these comments upset me, my friend says that grieving people don't just get better like they had the flu! This rationale is so logical and straightforward to me; it keeps me grounded and helps me realize that all the feelings I am experiencing are normal. I don't want to hear someone tell me what "stage" of grief I'm in or that everything happens for a reason and my life will be amazing again. I want someone to be honest and say things like "The fog in your brain won't even begin to lift for three years," or "Watch out for his friends because some of them won't be who you think they are." I need that person who can talk openly about the waves of anguish that overcome me at the most unexpected times, and who can feel my pain because they remember what each year marked for them. I want someone to laugh with me about all the insane things that have happened since and help me realize that none of it is bigger than me.

Sean was the love of my life, my soulmate, my only. There is no doubt in my mind about that. We were partners in every way, best friends, and as much as I wish we'd had so much more time together, I also know that we met at the exact time we were meant to meet. We were "ready" for each other. I owe a lot of thanks to him for what has become important to me in my life . . . not only because of losing him but also because of who he was when he was alive and because of who he allowed and encouraged me to be.

When we lose people we love, there are so many dips, dives, and turns on the new roller coaster of life. We question everything, wish for do-overs and, at times, wonder why they had to go. Why them? We think that they should be here and wonder why we are being punished in this life. What did we do to deserve this? It took me many months to get around these thoughts. Then, in a brief moment of undeniable clarity, I realized that losing Sean was not a punishment for something I had or hadn't done. Having him in my life was my reward.

Sarah Ozmond

Sarah Ozmond is an aspiring writer, connector, and friend to all beings. She has happily lived her entire life in various parts of Canada, and she now currently resides in Ontario.

Her deep love of travel has taken her a number of places throughout the world, and she will continue to see as much as she possibly can. Photography has also always been in Sarah's life, whether as part of her career or strictly for pleasure.

After experiencing a variety of significant life events including the loss of her partner, Sarah decided to share some of her story with the hope that it will help anyone out there starting, or currently on, their own journey through grief and discovery. She plans to use her writing and continuous sharing of experiences as ways to insert herself into people's lives when they need a friend. She believes the best way to connect is over a glass of wine while speaking honestly, having difficult conversations, and laughing at the most inappropriate times.

Among her peers, Sarah is known to be an excellent listener and someone with whom people can confide in and be ridiculous with. She has been told that anyone who meets her feels special and heard due to the inspirational attitude she brings to everything she does and that her story may be just what someone out there needs to hear.

You can get to know Sarah on her blog: mylifeafterdeathproject.com.

All the love and thanks to my incredibly supportive and compassionate family and to my amazing friends for getting me through this journey and continuing to do so, by whatever means necessary. To my sweet and patient little dog, Harpo, who no doubt has learned some creative and foul language through the process. And especially to my favourite human, my wonderful brother, Taylor, who like it or not, is stuck with me for eternity.

You are the greatest beings on the planet and this life is so much more fun for having you all in it.

She Is

——— Enough

CHAPTER 14

FIGHTING TO BELONG

Koa Baker

It feels like I have been at war with myself for my entire life. Fighting to belong. Fighting to be good enough. Fighting to have a place. Fighting to be loved. Fighting to be cared for. Fighting to show I am worthy. Fighting to be seen. I craved these things. I desperately wanted to feel as if someone just *saw* me. It felt as if I was always waving my arms: *"Look at me, listen to me, I am right here."* As I got older, I started to notice that I was seen when I looked a certain way. When I was thin, wearing cute clothes, makeup and hair perfect. I was seen and wanted. But sometimes it felt as if I was only seen because I was physically attractive. What was I without my body or my looks? Invisible. And feeling invisible wasn't an option for me. I already felt invisible to my family, even myself, and I needed to be seen. So, I grasped onto the only way I knew how and held onto it for dear life, fighting to keep it any way I could. I just didn't know at the time where it would lead me. I had no idea that I was learning to hate myself. I had no idea I was declaring war against myself.

∗ ∗ ∗

I am not sure when it started, the self-hate, but I know that it started when I was just a young girl. Everything and everyone around me told me how I was supposed to look, how my body was supposed to look. But I didn't look that way. I was taller, broader, thicker. My legs were longer, my thighs were bigger, my belly had a little extra to it, my arms were a little more jiggly. I wasn't small and petite like my friends, and I so desperately wanted to be like them. Those pretty girls with beautiful, thin legs in cute short skirts. The girls who looked incredible in their bathing suits when our school went to the pool for swimming lessons. I wanted to be them. As young as eight years old, I knew that I was expected to look like them if I wanted to be enough. Every movie, TV show, book, and magazine showed me how an ideal woman looked. I was inundated with images of the perfect women's bodies and how to achieve them. Yet, I didn't have that body, and I couldn't seem to get it. I never felt like I would be good enough unless I looked like those women on the TV or in the magazine. Not being "enough" carried with me throughout my childhood and into my teen years. I learned that pizza wasn't meant for girls like me. I learned that shorts were better saved for thinner women. I learned that belly shirts weren't cool on girls with a little extra, like me. I learned that bikinis weren't made for my body type. I learned that thinness made women desirable, beautiful, wanted. Thinness made women enough, and I wasn't thin. At least that is what I believed at the time. I believed I was overweight. I believed I was too big. I believed that no one would find me attractive. The thing is, though, no one actually ever said any of these things to me. No one ever told me I wasn't good enough because of my weight. No one ever indicated that I was overweight. I was only perpetuating this belief in myself. I was the one telling myself that I wasn't enough, and this feeling of not being enough consumed me. I learned that I wouldn't be enough unless I controlled how I looked, and I found that control in food, purging, punishing, restricting, and self-harm.

Binge, purge, restrict. Binge, purge, restrict. It felt like I was trapped in this cycle for most of my life. I would get to the point where I was so sick from losing weight that I didn't have the energy to get out of bed. I lost my period and was anemic, malnourished, and suffering, both physically and mentally.

I remember sitting on my kitchen floor. I was almost twenty pounds underweight, and I had no energy to even finish cooking dinner for my kids. I felt so weak, physically. I felt so low, mentally. I couldn't stop crying. I honestly wasn't sure if I was actually sick because I felt like I was barely alive. It was hard to lift my arms. I felt too weak to even get up. I called out to no one because no one was there, but it was a raw, deep, painful call for help. I had barely eaten that day, or days prior, because I convinced myself I needed to do a juice cleanse. This cleanse was just one of many. I was already underweight and barely fit into any of my clothes, but it wasn't enough. It wasn't enough because internally, I didn't feel like I was enough. I would push myself to the breaking point of dieting, hoping and wishing for some kind of wave of "ah, yes, there it is, I am now enough, a real woman." In reality, all I got was more suffering. I needed help so badly, but honestly, I don't think anyone even knew what I was going through. I was really good at pretending that I was okay, that I had it all together. No one around me knew I was suffering that way. Even my significant other, at the time, never knew that I was so sick. Looking back, I don't think I was ready for help. I didn't believe anything was wrong, even though I was suffering so badly. I didn't know that I was at war with my own body.

If it wasn't one war, it was another. I would try to gain control of myself and allow myself to eat. But eating meant bingeing. I would pretend to eat small amounts at dinner when I was around people, but I would stuff myself full while cooking when no one was watching. I stuffed myself because I was hungry, and I was hungry because I was restricting and purging. My body needed to eat, but I hated eating. I felt as if I lost control at these moments, like my body was forcing me to consume the calories it so badly needed. In the end, I would punish my body by purging again. I knew this cycle was all wrong, and so unhealthy, and I tried to stop. But then I would gain weight, and when I couldn't stand to see myself in the mirror anymore, I would try again to gain what I perceived as control. The purging would start. Laxatives were my go-to because they made me feel in control. I felt out of control with food and the fact that I had to eat every day, and laxatives gave me a sense of ridding myself of those calories. Even consuming healthy foods and calories was painful for me. I would eat as few calories as I could and still purge. Laxatives were easier than throwing up. No one noticed it. I could get away with it. But it wasn't enough. Because I still wasn't enough. I was still in pain, internally, and the bingeing and purging wasn't fixing it. So, I started numbing myself. Antidepressants. Ativan. Sleeping pills. Alcohol. Cutting. Anything to take away the pain inside. The pain of how much I hated myself. The pain of how much I disgusted myself.

Internally, I felt depressed. I was filled with so much sadness that I would cry myself to sleep at night. I would silently sob in the shower. I would cut myself just to feel something, anything other than mental pain and sadness. The cutting started when I was a teenager, then carried through to adulthood. It wasn't suicidal tendencies, it was about feeling. I cut my hands and thighs. Burned my skin. Poked holes in myself. Anything small enough to hide but deep enough to distract. The physical hurt was a relief from the mental hurt, and the mental hurt was too much to bear most days. I turned this pain on myself. I took it out on myself. It created an agony of living in this body that I loathed more than anything else in this world. I wasn't enough, and I never thought I would be enough, so why bother? Why bother caring about my body? Why bother caring about my health, my weight, my mind, my needs? Why bother when I will never ever be enough in this world?

Drinking was another easy way I numbed the pain—the mental pain that I was going through as well as the physical pain of not eating enough. It started innocently enough: a drink here and there, with friends or over dinner. The more I drank, the more I realized that it took away the pain, so I started drinking more and more. After a short time, I was buying mickeys or 26ers almost daily. I was drinking alone. Day or night. I tricked myself into thinking it was okay because I still kept up with my house and kids. I didn't get drunk until they were in bed. But while the drinking helped with the pain at first, it slowly enhanced my depression. I would slip into a drunken state of sadness, feeling hopeless and defeated. Ativan and antidepressants started to come in handy at that point. They were the only way I could fall asleep or function during the day without my mind spiralling out of control or falling to the floor in tears. I lived in a state of complete numbness for years.

✳ ✳ ✳

The problem with not feeling as if I were "enough" and always feeling self-hate was that I stopped caring about me. This self-hate carried on to adulthood, and I still struggle to this current day. I have done every diet, even the diets we pretend aren't diets, like veganism, or keto, or whatever new "perfect way of eating" comes up every year. I have done every new workout. I have tried every supplement and shake. I drank myself into an oblivion. I dulled myself with medications. But I never found my self-worth in any of those things.

I wish I could tell you that I am healed. That I have learned to love myself. That I no longer struggle with my relationship with food, my body, and myself. But those would all be lies. Because every day I still have to fight to not hate myself. I am still learning.

To this day, there is a bottle of laxatives in my medicine cabinet that I cannot bring myself to throw out. I look at it every night and tell myself that I don't need one. But I want one. I want to take one. I want to feel that emptiness in my stomach that makes me feel like maybe I am not as fat as I see myself. When I feel that emptiness, I feel like maybe I can eat that day without guilt. Maybe I can wear a tighter shirt. Wear my skinny jeans. Get naked in front of my husband without shame. Maybe if I can make myself feel thin, I can feel some kind of worth. Feeling full, like satisfied from a good meal, feels like pain. Feeling full feels like shame. Feeling full feels like I failed. Feeling full feels like I am disgusting. Feeling full means I am not thin. Not small enough. Not in control enough. Not good enough. Feeling full makes me feel fat. Fat. A word I hate and tell my kids not to use but something I feel every day. That bottle of laxatives takes away the fullness, that fatness. That bottle of laxatives makes me feel empty, and that emptiness makes me feel thin. Being thin makes me feel worthy—worthy of this life, of love, of admiration. And so I look at that bottle of laxatives, and I desperately want to take one, even though I know not to anymore. But I still want to, because learning to love yourself doesn't happen quickly. Learning to love yourself doesn't happen when you stop punishing yourself. Learning to love yourself is so much harder than I ever thought possible. Learning that my worth is not tied to the size of my body, well, that is a work in progress.

I still look at myself in the mirror and assess every little part of my body. Did my belly grow? Do my arms jiggle? Can I see more cellulite in my thighs? I squish and poke and shake every part of my body, looking for change. Even though my clothes still fit, I want my clothes to be too big; I want to see myself shrinking. Any growth on my body feels like a failure, so much so that I internally feel as if I failed at something huge and monumental, when in reality, my body just changed and expanded. When I see the extra fat or weight, I feel completely hopeless and helpless, as if I am at the mercy of a body that hates me. Why doesn't it listen to me? "Be thinner," "Don't gain any weight," "Work out harder!" And it doesn't listen to me. My body fails me over and over. At least, that is what I have told myself. But the truth is, my body isn't failing me. I am failing me. I am the one failing my body. I have put my body through so much pain and torment, striving for something impossible to obtain: acceptance by a society that will always find more to criticize. I thought I needed that acceptance to finally be free, free from the pain. If that is what I am basing my worth on, the standards of a society that are based on unrealistic ideologies and expectations, I will never be enough. I have had to change who I am striving to be accepted by, and the only person who needs to accept me, is me.

I am still learning to change these behaviours and accept myself. But change is hard. For a long time, I thought I could do it alone. I would read books on self-improvement. I would avoid eating triggers and allow myself to eat, but it never stuck. I have had to seek out counselling from someone who is an expert with disordered eating. I have had to learn that I need to change my entire mindset. It isn't just learning to eat, it is learning that your mind is disordered and needs help. Learning to love yourself and accept yourself is hard, especially when you have allowed external forces to dictate your worth. Seeing myself gain weight is hard. I had to watch my weight jump all over the place, up and down. I had to buy new clothes, as my "skinny" clothes no longer fit. I had to learn to eat, and I had to learn that getting enough calories was necessary. I had to learn that rolls and squishy spots on my body are normal. I had to learn that it is okay that I have cellulite on my thighs. Stretch marks are normal! I had to learn that it is okay if you can't see my ribs or my collarbone. I had to learn that I can indulge in food without having to do extra cardio to make up for it. I had to throw out diets and food control. I cannot cleanse, or cut carbs, or weigh food. I cannot buy those diet shakes or work-outs guaranteeing weight loss in only a few short weeks. I cannot weigh myself, measure myself, or look at my body in the mirror if I am having a bad mental health day. I cannot avoid weight gain, or loss, or the ups and downs that are normal for us to go through. I cannot do these things because they are triggers, they are harmful, they are dysfunctional and disordered, but society—diet culture—says they are normal. It is hard to fight an entire culture that puts worth on women based on being a certain size or shape.

I am still learning, but now I am fighting to feel as if I am enough and I belong, within myself.

Brené Brown says it perfectly:

> *True belonging is the spiritual practice of believing in and belonging to yourself so deeply that you can share your authentic self with the world . . . True belonging doesn't require you to change who you are; it requires you to be who you are.*[1]

What I have learned is that my struggle has never been about my body. I have been fighting to feel "enough" my whole life, and I related my "enoughness" to my looks, to my body. I have tried so hard to feel like I belong to something, anything. I didn't want to feel like I was an outsider, like I didn't have a place. Society told me that my worth was in my beauty and my body, and I consumed those lies and lived them for thirty-four years. I let those lies destroy me and bring me to my knees, to my breaking point. But those lies are now my strength. They are what I am fighting every day. I fight to change those lies, to not only stop believing them myself but to teach young girls and other women that they, too, can stop believing those lies. My worth has never been tied to my body. My worth has never been tied to my weight. My feelings of being enough, feelings of belonging, aren't about anything other than me, and that means you are also enough, just as you are, in this moment. So, do I actually believe that I am enough for myself? Do I actually believe that I only need to belong to myself? Maybe not fully yet, but I am trying. I no longer look for my worth in my body, or from society.

Belonging. Worth. Acceptance. Self-love. Gaining these is the purpose for the war. It was never about how my body looked. It was never about how my legs looked in shorts, or how my belly looked in a bikini. This war was never about my weight, my measurements, my ability to stay slim and trim. No, this war was never about my body. It was about finding myself. It was about loving myself, as I am. It was about feeling as if I am enough, enough in every way. It was about learning that I do have a place in this world, and I do belong, and if not to a specific group, I belong to myself. I am good enough for *myself*. I had to stop fighting, I had to lay down the white flag and submit to everything I thought I was fighting in order to see that this war was always about finding out that I was always enough. At least now I know that I have always been enough, I just needed to see it in myself.

Koa Baker

Koa Baker has spent years standing out as a female executive in the male-dominated construction industry. Koa, along with her husband, founded Duffy Baker Construction Corp. She fiercely took on the role as chief of operations. Construction wasn't her calling, and she has since put her entrepreneurial skills to work by turning herself into an online business.

Koa is a self-made content creator, blogger, published author, and self-love and mental health advocate. She spends most of her days pounding away on her computer, writing books, blogs, and growing her Instagram following.

Koa's formal education came in the form of a bachelor's degree with a double major in Psychology and Indigenous Studies. Koa is also in the process of training to be a registered counsellor with a specialization in addictions. Koa uses her education to help her better understand how to help men and women face and overcome their own adversity.

Adversity is something Koa knows well. Before becoming an executive, author, and content creator, Koa had been lost; she was hopelessly adrift in a sea of abuse, trauma, limiting beliefs, diet culture punishment, and mental illness diagnoses. An unhappy combination of medication and booze kept her afloat. Through immense growth, Koa has taken on the belief that she was allowing all her adversity to take place and in order to grow, she had to become her own solution. Now, Koa spends much of her time advocating for others who suffer with mental illness as well as from the damages of diet culture. Through normalizing mental illness, as well as normalizing real bodies, she has grown her Instagram from a mere 300 to over 11,000 in only a couple months. Through her real, raw, and emotional Instagram posts, Koa inspires thousands of others to embrace their true selves.

Thank you to my husband, Duffy, for always supporting me, encouraging me, and cheering me on. You have helped me grow into the best version of myself. Without you, life wouldn't be the same.

FINAL WORDS

The journey to creating this book didn't come easily for the authors. Countless days were spent frustrated, emotional, and uncertain, because sharing the rawest parts of ourselves is so much harder than we could ever imagine. But these authors did it anyway. They pushed through all their pain and discomfort and were able to create something beautiful. They pushed through because they knew that they needed to stand strong for you.

My hope is that after reading this book, you feel inspired, uplifted, empowered, and seen. You are not alone; you have a collective of women who are just like you and who understand you. I hope you know now that you, too, can overcome any kind of adversity that is thrown at you.

I am so incredibly proud of the women who stepped up to share their truths in these stories, and I am so incredibly proud of you for picking up this book and becoming a part of the Great Canadian Woman sisterhood.

END NOTES

Jennifer McKenney

1. Carl Jung Quotes. Goodreads. https://www.goodreads.com/quotes/44379-until-you-make-the-unconscious-conscious-it-will-direct-your, accessed May 23, 2021.

2. Maya Angelou Quotes. Goodreads. https://www.goodreads.com/quotes/120991-you-alone-are-enough-you-have-nothing-to-prove-to, accessed May 27, 2021.

3. Williamson, Marianne. *A Return to Love: Reflections on the Principles of "A Course of Miracles."* HarperOne, 1996.

Amy Brookes

1. Dunne, Griffin, dir. *Practical Magic.* Warner Bros., 1998.

Joan of Arc Quotes. BrainyQuote.com, BrainyMedia Inc, 2021. https://www.brainyquote.com/quotes/joan_of_arc_193094, accessed May 23, 2021.

Julie Brooks

1. Bernstein, Gabrielle. *Super Attractor: Methods for Manifesting a Life beyond Your Wildest Dreams.* Hay House, 2021.

2. Gautama Buddha Quotes. Goodreads. https://www.goodreads.com/quotes/3181192-in-the-end-only-three-things-matter-how-much-you, accessed May 23, 2021.

Koa Baker

1. Brown, Brené. *Braving the Wilderness: The Quest for True Belonging and the Courage to Stand Alone.* Random House, 2017.

We aren't your average publisher! GCW Publishing House and Media Group™ is a Canadian woman-owned and operated publishing house where we ignite courage and confidence in women worldwide and help them write high-impact, non-fiction books that make waves, move mountains, blaze trails, and change lives! We combine the art of storytelling, connection, camaraderie, support, marketing, and public relations into the book-writing experience to provide our authors with the entire publishing process and beyond!

For more information on publishing, blogging, and podcasting opportunities, please visit: gcwpublishing.com

THE GREAT CANADIAN WOMAN — SHE IS STRONG AND FREE SERIES

An inspiring three-volume series of real-life stories from Canadian women who have overcome life adversities, found a way through seemingly impossible circumstances, and rose above their pain and tribulations. Their courageous stories will instil a sense of hope and empowerment in others so that they, too, can overcome their personal hardships and know they are not alone. These stories grant us all the permission to live fully, love deeply, and fight like hell in the name of happiness.

THE GREAT CANADIAN WOMAN— SHE IS STRONG AND FREE I

The Great Canadian Woman is all of us. She is the single mother who provides for her children come hell or high water. She is the woman who has a dream and musters up enough courage to go after it. She is the woman who has quarreled in the depths of pain and grief and finds her way back home to herself. She is the woman who says no to what does not serve her. She is the woman who says enough is enough and commits to a new way of living. She is the woman who finds the strength to leave toxic relationships. She is the woman who knows unconditional love. She is the woman who takes the lead and lights the torch. She is the woman who refuses to accept the limits that someone else placed before her. She is the woman who knocks down doors and shatters glass ceilings. She is the woman who finds a way out of no way then turns around, extends her hand, and brings as many people as she can along with her. These stories grant us all the permission to live fully, love deeply, and fight like hell in the name of happiness.

THE GREAT CANADIAN WOMAN— SHE IS STRONG AND FREE II

The Great Canadian Woman is every woman. She is overcoming trauma. She is coming to terms with her intuition. She is changing careers and finding a new path. She is grieving while raising her children. She is overcoming racial injustices. She is removing mental health stigmas. She is finding her joy. She is raw and real. She is a light in the darkness. She stumbles and falls, but she rises by sharing her story and speaking her truth. Sometimes we need to break so we can rebuild. In the chapters of this book, these great Canadian women show you how to do just that, through their intense vulnerability, massive strength, immense courage, and endless perseverance.

SHE SERIES AND HER SPECIAL EDITION SISTER SERIES

A collection of real-life stories from courageous women around the globe who confidently share their life experiences. Whether they have overcome life traumas, found a way through seemingly impossible circumstances, or embarked on the often turbulent entrepreneurial path, they have all bravely risen above their pain and fears. They no longer hide behind their own or other people's judgment but forge ahead, speaking their truth, making waves, moving mountains, and blazing trails while being the leaders they were always meant to be.